CONTRAST

CONTRAST

An Investigator's Basic Reference Guide to Fingerprint Identification Concepts

By

CRAIG A. COPPOCK

Charles C Thomas
PUBLISHER • LTD.
SPRINGFIELD • ILLINOIS • U.S.A.

Published and Distributed Throughout the World by

CHARLES C THOMAS • PUBLISHER, LTD.
2600 South First Street
Springfield, Illinois 62704

ISBN 0-398-07130-6 (cloth)
ISBN 0-398-07131-4 (paper)

Library of Congress Catalog Card Number: 00-061531

With THOMAS BOOKS *careful attention is given to all details of manufacturing
and design. It is the Publisher's desire to present books that are satisfactory as to their
physical qualities and artistic possibilities and appropriate for their particular use.*
THOMAS BOOKS *will be true to those laws of quality that assure a good name
and good will.*

Printed in the United States of America
CJ-R-3

Library of Congress Cataloging-in-Publication Data

Coppock, Craig A.
  Contrast : an investigator's basic reference guide to fingerprint
identification concepts / by Craig A. Coppock.
    p. cm.
  Includes bibliographical references and index.
  ISBN 0-398-07130-6 -- ISBN 0-398-07131-4 (pbk.)
    1. Fingerprints--Identification. I. Title.

HV6074 .C63 2000
363.25'8--dc21
                                                    00-061531

PREFACE

Contrast is a new approach in the instruction of basic fingerprint identification concepts. Currently, most persons referencing fingerprint information will find out-of-date information or that which only an experienced fingerprint specialist could appreciate. I have compiled the information for *Contrast* during the teaching of fingerprint science to; criminal justice students, new crime scene investigators, and to experienced patrol officers.

While it is easy to write chapters detailing fingerprint identification's history and classification details, it is difficult to present logical arguments for simple identification concepts. *Contrast* is written to present conceptual ideas in context with the basics of fingerprint science. This book is designed to be read in its entirety or to be reference as a guidebook, as many concepts and information are repeated and cross-referenced. The information helps the reader to understand the relationships, benefits, and limitations of crime scene fingerprint evidence.

Craig A. Coppock

INTRODUCTION

The science of fingerprint identification is fast becoming technology oriented. Gone are the days of simplistic modus operandi, and going is the day of police officer duty rotation that includes fingerprint identification. Most law enforcement agencies are converting their identification bureau's staffing from commissioned officers to full-time civilian operations. Yet, most of these civilian identification bureaus are still managed and funded by the law enforcement agency for which they work. This allows the continuing training of the fingerprint specialist while being able to provide investigative and support services to the agency.

Fingerprint specialists can be found performing fingerprint identification work on crime scenes, jail inmate identification, job applicant criminal background checks, immigration identification, criminal records verification, and routine identification for the public. Fingerprint identification has a reputation for reliability and accuracy. In fingerprint identification, names mean almost nothing. Many persons have so many alias names they could not possibly remember them all. For most law enforcement documentation purposes, it is only the first name ever given that is used for reference. This first gave name in conjunction with fingerprinting is considered a true name. All others would be considered an alias and would be referenced to the true name. The reason for this is that while names may change, the identification value of a fingerprint does not.

The science of fingerprint identification is one of the few scientific disciplines that does not routinely require college-degreed apprentices.[1] However, the fingerprint specialist does rely on a wide variety of related scientific disciplines, such as chemistry, physics, biology, mathematics, and photography. A good understanding of fundamental statistics is also beneficial.

---

1. The science of fingerprints has evolved into a applied science with multiple scientific aspects supporting actual fingerprint identification.

A fingerprint specialist cannot afford to suffer from innumeracy.[2] The reason for this is the concept that while no two objects are identical except in source, under some circumstances, items that are sufficiently similar may cause identification difficulties. This concept is later discussed in detail.

On the average, it takes about five years of training and fieldwork to be considered a proficient and experienced fingerprint specialist. One of the reasons for this is that most difficult fingerprint identifications demand experience. While it is unnecessary for an expert to have years of experience to make a fingerprint identification, inexperience may result in misidentifications and a higher than average number of *missed identifications*. A *misidentification* is a false positive or false identification. With a misidentification, the compared fingerprint impressions are not of identical origin. A missed identification is simply an unrecognized identification. It is standard practice that any fingerprint identifications made from crime scene fingerprints are verified by another qualified fingerprint specialist. This verification process is the foundation of the high-quality work the fingerprint identification field has bestowed upon itself.

In general, fingerprint specialists pride themselves on being unbiased and ethical in their professionalism. While it may sometimes seem otherwise, fingerprint identifications are founded from the evidence itself, not from suggestions by other investigators. There is no room for guesswork or speculation with fingerprint identifications. If latent crime scene fingerprints were developed, were they identified? If the answer is that no identifications have been made, why not?

The fingerprint specialist carries a considerable amount of responsibility. Most persons, as well as employers, *demand* that he or she be 100% error free regarding fingerprint identifications. This degree of accuracy is not expected from the vast majority of other professions, both within and outside the judicial system. A fingerprint examiner who is not accurate with his or her fingerprint identifications will find himself or herself immediately unemployable in the field of fingerprint identification.

This guidebook illustrates the basic concepts involved in the science of fingerprints and fingerprint identification. *Contrast* is intend-

---

2. Innumeracy, the lack of mathematical comprehension on its most basic level, was brought to light in John Allen Paulos's book *Innumeracy: Mathematical Illiteracy and Its Consequences* New York: Hill and Wang, 1988.

ed for new and experienced crime scene investigators, patrol officers, attorneys, and students who seek to add fingerprint identification to their investigative skills. To understand fingerprint identification, a person needs to see through the confusing generalities to fingerprint identification's underlying concepts.

ACKNOWLEDGMENTS

I am grateful for the generous suggestions and input by Eric Berg of the Tacoma Police Department's Forensics Unit, and Dorothy Blyton of the Spokane Sheriff's Identification Unit, retired. I have relied on their input to keep *Contrast* focused and effective. I have long known that the more I consult my peers for new perspectives and ideas, the better a project will be. This book is no exception.

It is hoped that *Contrast: An Investigator's Basic Reference Guide to Fingerprint Identification Concepts* will help clarify many of the over simplified generalities that pervade the science of fingerprint identification. Also, it is my intention to highlight the many possibilities and limitations of fingerprint identification. If these goals are achieved, I will have been successful this endeavor.

I dedicate this book to my family.

CONTENTS

CONTRAST

Chapter 1

FINGERPRINTS IN CONTEXT

1. INTRODUCTION TO FINGERPRINTS

Welcome to the science of fingerprint identification or *dactylography*.[1] The word fingerprint is a generic term for all the friction ridges located on the palmar surface of the hands and the soles of the feet. Although actual fingerprints only include the friction ridge detail after the last joint on each finger or impressions thereof, it is common to hear the term fingerprint used as an all-encompassing generality. The term fingerprint is also being used as a generality for other types of identification as well. This may include such unusual wordage as DNA fingerprint identification. Of course, the actual meaning is that a DNA identification is an effective means of identification as is fingerprint identification. This kind of generality is not an acceptable practice by fingerprint experts when giving court testimony. A properly trained fingerprint identification specialist must give specific details as to the location and nature of the fingerprint evidence while speaking in layman's terms.

While certain genetic impairments can prevent the formation of friction ridges during the embryonic development stage, this kind of impairment and other ridge development problems, such as dysplasia, are very rare. Dysplasia is a defect in the development of the friction skin ridge detail that is noticeable as fragmented friction ridges.

---

1. Dactyloscopy is an alternate term used for the science of fingerprint identification. Its origin is from the Greek word "daktulos" or finger. However, modern dactylography covers all friction skin based identification, not just the fingers.

Most all *Homo sapiens* exhibit friction ridge detail on the gripping surfaces of the hands and feet. Other primates can also have these friction ridges on their gripping surfaces. Some primates are even known to have friction ridges on the underside of the tail near the base (Berry, 1991). The genetic aspects of friction ridges are obvious, though the genetics have not been studied in great detail.

Fingerprinting as a means of identification is a relatively recent phenomenon. Only in the last 100 years have inked fingerprint impressions been recorded routinely en masse as a positive means of identification. Each method of identification utilizes the differences found when comparing two items or persons. Some alternate means of identification, both historical and modern, can include the following sample list.

•Alternate forms identification:
•Tattooing
•Photography
•Anthropometry[2]
•Deoxyribonucleic acid (DNA)
•Retinal scans (via computer imaging)[3]
•Ear identification (ear impressions)
•Dental records (x-ray images containing teeth characteristics)

Yet, unlike these options, fingerprinting a person with regular printer's type ink is simple, efficient, and standardized. Checking a person's identification against a previously recorded fingerprint impression halfway around the world is as simple as sending a high resolution fax or other digital image over a phone line.

A fingerprint specialist is a person who is trained in the science of fingerprint documentation, crime scene fingerprint development, and fingerprint identification. A fingerprint specialist can compare friction skin impressions for specific likeness to determine if the separate impressions were made by one and the same source. Persons in the scientific field of fingerprint identification are labeled with a variety of names such as fingerprint examiner, identification officer, identifica-

---

2. Anthropometry is a body measurement system developed by Alphonse Bertillon (1853-1914).

3. Eyeglass prescriptions are also noted to be very unique to each individual. However, in large populations the uniqueness may not be statistically sufficient due to the specific increments used in corrective adjustments.

tion technician, forensic specialist, latent print examiner, or finger-print specialist.[4] The actual job titles vary regionally and even local-ly, among agencies. Since this book is intended to be a general fin-gerprint concept reference book, the generalized name of *fingerprint specialist* will be used as opposed to other specific titles. Note that a fingerprint specialist may also be competent in other related fields such as crime scene evidence processing; photography and videogra-phy documentation: tool mark, shoe, and tire tread examination; as well as other forensic specialties such as chemistry.

The concept of fingerprint identification is twofold. First is that no two fingerprint impressions are identical, except possibly, in their source. Second the relative positions of the friction skin characteris-tics do not change over the course of a person's life.[5] To quote the poet Elliott Allen Baade, "Identical, when not one in the same, is sim-ilar" (Baade, 1998, p. 78), the idea being that the closer you look at two or more tangible objects or persons, the more differences you will find.[6] For a forensic identification application, this can be trans-lated to: no two tangible objects are identical except in source. A forensic identification requires that certain words must be qualified in meaning to ensure that any scientific conclusion is not misunder-stood. Thus, identical cannot mean similar and similar cannot possi-bly mean identical. Many forms of identification are based on this concept.

Imagine blue and white aluminum soft drink cans rolling off the assembly line by the thousands. From a distance they all look the same; yet, on closer inspection, we see many differences, such as the drink opening lines up with the label differently on each can. Look closer and we notice the aluminum surface has variations; it is not perfectly smooth. If you were to take one of these soft drink cans and empty its contents into two different glasses, we could say that the liq-uid in each glass is identical regarding its source. The cola originated from an identical cola can and from an identical secret formula. For

---

4. While criminal investigation may be an "art," fingerprint identification is a statistically-based, applied science.

5. Scarring or other permanent damage to the friction skin of the hands or feet does not gen-erally pose problems for fingerprint identification.

6. Nontangible items such as letters or numbers are indeed identical. A number 7, for example, is always a number 7. In reality, the word "identical" could have several inferred meanings; however, for fingerprint identification, the word identical is meant in reference to a source for friction skin impressions. Also, the spatial relationships of specific points of identification may also be identical, meaning that they originated from an identical source.

the aluminum cans themselves, we could say that all the cans originated from the same assembly line. The soda cans originated from an identical source.

The concept that no two tangible objects are identical can even be taken down to near the quantum physics level to Heisenberg's uncertainty principle. In Heisenberg's indefinable quantum world, our classical laws and logic do not apply. Of course, fingerprint identification need not go this far.

The effectiveness and reliability of fingerprint identification are based on sound principles and statistics that no two fingerprints are sufficiently similar that they may be mistaken as being identical. In other words, no two fingerprints are alike.[7] Nature does not repeat itself. Each of nature's products contains its own unique characteristics. These characteristics are the details of identification.

A very important point to remember, regarding fingerprint identification, is that a developed latent crime scene fingerprint and an inked fingerprint are never exactly the same in appearance. Indeed, one fingerprint impression is made of ink and the other by some development process or of a photographic image. Yet, these two impressions may be from an identical source, such as a finger, palm, or the sole of a foot. Recall the aluminum cans rolling off the assembly line, each can has its unique details.

No two different fingers have ever been found to make an identical impression. Nor would logic expect it to be otherwise, because even slight differences in fingerprint detail can be recognized to differentiate between individual fingerprints. Since the fingers are all connected to the palm and the friction skin covers the palmar side of the hand from the tip of the finger to the wrist we really have only four impression sources, two palmar and two plantar surfaces. The plantar area's friction skin is similar to the hands. With the addition of some creases, the friction skin is continuous from the toes to the heel (see also Chapter 2).

Inked fingerprints are also called exemplar prints or known prints. Once a set of these known impressions is available, then other fingerprint impressions can be compared to this known file. For most felonies, several sets of fingerprints can be taken.[8] These 10-print

7. This refers to the friction skin itself, not to impressions made by the same area of friction skin.

8. Additional fingerprint or footprint impressions may be taken depending on case or employment requirements.

cards, as they are known, are then filed with the different governmental branches(see Fig. 1). If a person is booked into the jail of a town or city, the fingerprint cards may include distribution these other agencies. Depending on the local requirements, a 10-print fingerprint card may be retained into local, state/province, and national files. A national file in the United States would include the fingerprint files of the Federal Bureau of Investigation (FBI). The state and FBI will report back to the originating agency if a match is found with a fingerprint file in their system. A criminal history or identification history is based on these fingerprint files. Different names that are used are listed as alias names in addition to the *original* name on the first fingerprint card filed. All future 10-print fingerprint cards are intended to be combined via fingerprint comparisons with other existing fingerprint files. This is to ensure a common history file for all identical fingerprint cards. It is possible that errors can be made that would prevent the matching of all identical cards to the same history file.

Possible Errors in Consolidation of Criminal History Files Based on Fingerprint Identification

• Clerical error.
• 10-print files or individual criminal history files were combined without a positive fingerprint identification confirming that all files were of the same person.
• Not all the various government files were located for fingerprint comparison.
• Fingerprint identification error.

2. A BRIEF HISTORY OF FINGERPRINT IDENTIFICATION

The widespread use of fingerprinting as a means of identification occurred after 1900.[9] The previous methods of identification were

9. For several millennia, people have been aware that fingerprints exist, and that they vary in their details. Yet only in the last few hundred years has friction skin been studied in scientific detail.

inefficient and problematic. One of the turning points that allowed fingerprint identification to be utilized as the primary means of identification occurred at the Leavenworth, Kansas prison in 1903. In this case, two men, William West, and Will West shared a similar Bertillon body measurement formula. However, comparison of their fingerprint impressions revealed their different identities. The Bertillon system was at that time a main source of identifying individuals (FBI, page 11).

In 1880, Dr. Henry Faulds had written a scientific paper on the identification possibilities of fingerprints. Dr. Faulds had also demonstrated the concept of fingerprint identification using actual latent fingerprints. This interest in fingerprints by Faulds was expanded by Englishman Francis Galton (1822-1911).[10] Galton was the first to introduce a book on the subject of fingerprints and of their identification value. Following Galton's book, several other persons devised classification schemes to retrieve a filed 10-print fingerprint card from a collection of hundreds or thousands. One of these fingerprint classification systems was developed by Sir Edward Henry in 1897. This new Henry classification system was a further improvement on Galton's work. Even today, in our computerized world, most file systems use some elements of the Henry classification system.

Another workable classification system was developed by an Argentinean, Dr. Juan Vucetich (1858-1925). Vucetich's system predates Henry's and was also based on Galton's fingerprint research. Versions of Dr. Vucetich's fingerprint classification system are still in use in some Spanish-speaking countries (Saferstein, 1990 & *FBI Advanced Latent Fingerprint Manual*). In the 1940s, there were about fifty different versions of fingerprint classification. Many of these later classification systems were expansions on existing systems such as the Vucetich system or the Henry system.

The manual file Henry system was only recently replaced as the filing classification system of choice. Today, with millions of fingerprint files being generated, a faster more efficient system was needed. In the mid to late 1970s, the computer revolution reached the science of fingerprint classification and identification. Computers have drastically changed the effectiveness of the fingerprint identification field. A computer can generate a candidate list of possible matches in just

---

10. Francis Galton was a cousin of the famous naturalist Charles Darwin (1809-1882).

minutes after searching the extensive fingerprint databases of local, regional, and national governments. Today's fingerprint databases contain fingerprint impressions from criminal as well as civil sources. (See Chapter 11 for more information on computerized fingerprint databases.)

Sample of Fingerprint Database and Fingerprint File Sources

- Criminal arrests with fingerprints taken during booking.
- Government employees including criminal justice applications.
- Miscellaneous public applications.
- Private and commercial licenses.
- Immigration/aliens.
- Personal identification; including investigative and voluntary submissions.

Many criminal history checks that are verified with fingerprints do not generate a permanent fingerprint record. In these cases, once a search of various computerized fingerprint databases has been completed, the search results and related 10-print cards are returned to the requester or destroyed[11] (see Fig. 1 and 20 for versions of 10-print cards). Search results are simply computer generated candidate lists of possible fingerprint matches. For verification, an actual fingerprint comparison of a possible matching candidate would be made by the fingerprint specialist who initiated the database search. Local and national laws will likely determine if an agency can or need to retain a fingerprint file permanently.

----

11. Some computerized fingerprint databases do not need an inked fingerprint to affect a database search. These paperless systems rely on a digital image of a fingerprint impression and electronic file management of related personal information.

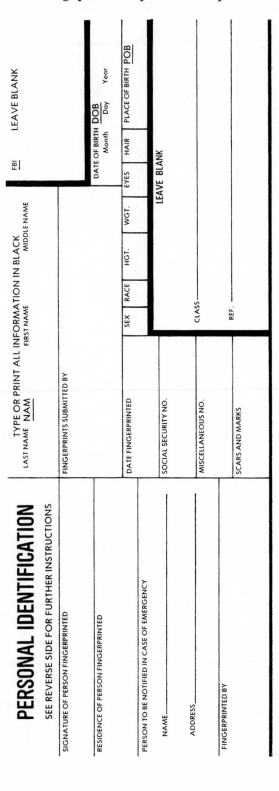

Figure 1a. Standardized format personal identification 10-print card.

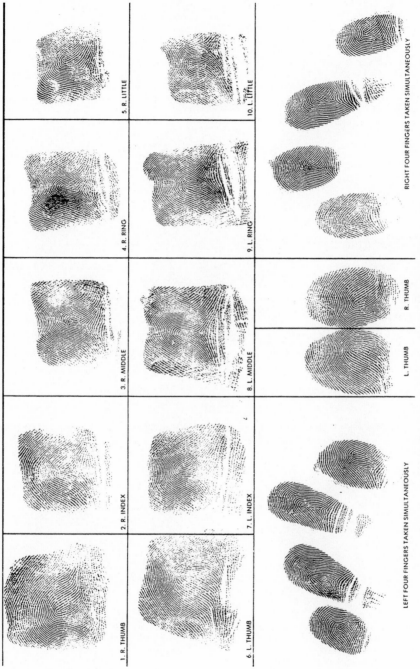

Figure 1b. Standardized format personal identification 10-print card.

Chapter 2

FRICTION SKIN

1. WHAT ARE FINGERPRINTS?

Fingerprints are friction ridge skin or papillary ridges that are found on the palmar surface and soles of the feet. Friction skin is analogous to geologic ridges and valleys where the valleys represent the area between the raised area of skin. The concept of friction ridges as a gripping skin is analogous to the tread of an automotive tire. Friction skin consists of a structured dermis layer with the friction structure, including sweat pores, extending up though the epidermis layer of the skin (see Fig. 4). The edges of the ridges cause increased friction as contact and shear pressures are applied.

Friction skin also has an enhanced quantity of nerves and pores. The extra nerves found on the palmar surface allows for extra sensory feedback to the brain. This feedback helps us better control the

Figure 2. Inked palm print (not to scale).   Figure 3. Inked foot print (not to scale).

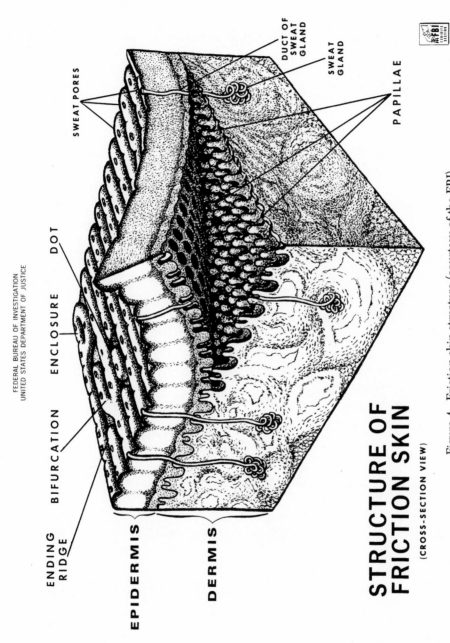

Figure 4. Friction skin structure (courtesy of the FBI).

articulation of our hands, especially when dealing with small objects. The extra pores that line the friction ridges allow the friction skin to remain moist and this keeps the skin soft and pliable. Softer, pliable friction skin offers better frictional characteristics.

We are born with our friction skin detail fully developed. The *spatial relationships* of characteristics within the ridge detail do not change as we grow. (See section 1-A in this chapter for descriptions of identifying characteristics.) Since identifications are based on the spatial relationships of the ridge characteristics, comparing different sizes of impressions is of no concern. An analogy of size differences would be like a single photographic negative enlarged to various sizes. The information in the photographs remains the same no matter what size it is.[1] Large differences in size are usually only found when comparing a small child's fingerprint or footprint to an adult. It is possible that a fingerprint search of a computer database may miss a fingerprint match if the size difference between the file print and the search print is outside certain size parameters. However, this rarely seems to be an issue.

Scars and severe burns can obliterate sections of friction skin, but the damaged area must also include the underlying dermis layer of the skin to have any permanent effect on the topmost epidermis layer. This is because friction skin ridge structure resides in, and is generated from, the dermis layer.

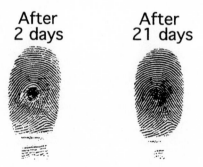

Figure 5. Superficial burn to friction skin epidermis layer.

1. Perspective would be an exception when photographic sizes change. A true perspective results in the two-dimensional re-creation of specific size and spatial relationships. This information is only relevant for re-creating certain view perspectives and has no bearing on fingerprint identification.

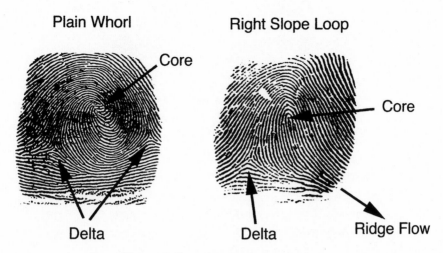

Figure 6. Basic fingerprint anatomy

Most minor burns, blisters, and warts only affect the top-most epidermis layer of the skin. The normal healing process gradually replaces the epidermis layer with new skin. This new skin will again reflect the ridge structure of the dermis layer. Millions of dead skin cells are shed each day, with millions more replacing those in a continuous process of skin renewal. The underlying, dermis-based, friction skin will replace the damaged area with friction ridges identical to the original.[2] Damage to the underlying dermis layer that does result in permanent damage to the friction skin and to the spatial relationships in the ridge detail are explainable differences. Explainable differences do not generally pose any problems when making fingerprint comparisons and identifications.[3]

A. Basic Fingerprint Pattern Types

Patterns are general friction ridge features that give a fingerprint its shape. Pattern types are groups of similar-shaped fingerprints or fingerprint impressions. There are three major categories for eight pattern types (see Figs. 7, 8, & 9). Each category has subcategories that

---

2. The term identical is in reference to regenerated skin. The new epidermis layer is generated from the identical dermis source, and the spatial relationships of characteristics in this new epidermis layer will continue to reflect the detail of the dermis.

3. Reference Chapter 8, Concepts of Fingerprint Identification, for more information on explainable differences.

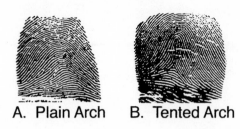

A. Plain Arch   B. Tented Arch

Figure 7. Arches (arches comprise about 5% of all pattern types).

group patterns according to established divisional rules used in the Henry classification system. In this section, a brief overview of the three major categories will be discussed (see also Appendix A for historical and computerized fingerprint pattern terms).

The simplest pattern type is the arch. The arch pattern is further divided into two separate pattern forms, the plain arch and the tented arch. The plain arch is generally a side-to-side flow of ridges with an unremarkable arch near the center of the pattern. The tented arch will typically possess a ridge structure that deviates from the side-to-side arch flow with an up-thrust of ridges that angle 45 degrees or more (FBI, 1984, pp. 30-33) (see Fig. 7).

Loop patterns can also be described as ulnar and radial if they are referenced from a hand or 10-print fingerprint card, as it would then be known which hand made the impression. As seen in impression form, the predominant ulnar loop has a direction of ridge flow that proceeds toward the ulnar bone in the arm therefore, they are called ulnar loops. The same can be said for the less common radial loop, except its ridges would tend to flow to the side of the arm with the radial bone (see Fig. 8). However, if it is unknown which hand, left or right, made the impression, then the impressions are simply called left or right flowing, sloping, or slanting loops. These three terms are all used interchangeably. Technically, for a fingerprint pattern to be classified as a loop, the pattern must meet a set of requirements. The requirements for the loop pattern are as follows:

Loop Pattern Requirements:

• A sufficient recurve must be present. A recurve is generally the core area of a fingerprint pattern.
• A delta must be present in the pattern.
• A ridge count, of at least one ridge, must cross a looping (recurv-

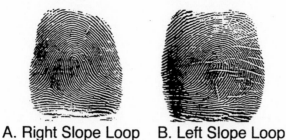

A. Right Slope Loop   B. Left Slope Loop

Figure 8. Loops (loops comprise about 65% of all pattern types).

ing) ridge. The ridge count is taken in the area between the delta and the core.

These basic requirements are further refined with specific requirements for a recurve, a delta, the ridge count itself, and the core (FBI, 1984, p. 18). The loop pattern, as well as the other patterns of the arch and the whorl must also meet specific requirements in order to be classified as a particular pattern type. If all requirements of a loop are not met, the fingerprint will be assigned another pattern type depending on its features. A detailed description of these pattern typing requirements is found in the FBI's book, *The Science of Fingerprints*.

The third major category for fingerprint pattern types is the whorl. The whorl category is divided into four pattern types: the plain whorl, central pocket whorl, double loop, and accidental whorl (see Fig. 9). Each of these whorl pattern types has specific requirements. The basic definition of a whorl-type pattern is that at least two deltas are present with a recurve in front of each delta (FBI, 1984, p. 45). The whorl patterns can be further classified with a tracing of the

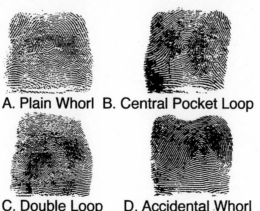

A. Plain Whorl B. Central Pocket Loop

C. Double Loop   D. Accidental Whorl

Figure 9. Whorls (whorls comprise about 30% of all pattern types).

ridges between the left-most delta and the right-most delta. Basic
tracing requirements are that the ridges are followed to the right until
a point nearest the right-most delta is reached. The location of this
nearest point will determine if the whorl is of a inner, outer, or meet
type of tracing. With an inner traced whorl, the traced point on the
ridge nearest the right-most delta is three or more ridges inside the
pattern area from the delta. With outer-traced whorls, the nearest
point to the delta arrived at by tracing is three or more ridges from
the right-most delta outside the pattern area. A meet tracing is that
nearest point that is within three ridges either side of the right delta.

This description is simply an overview of the pattern basics.
Classification of pattern types requires many details to ensure that
each pattern will fit into a particular pattern type. If a fingerprint pattern does not fall into one of the regular categories, then it must be
labeled as an accidental whorl or a scar, if need be. Most patterns are
easily categorized and pattern typed. Accidental whorls represent
only a small percentage of whorl pattern types. The pattern designation of scar is reserved for impressions that contain excessive scaring
that obliterate the pattern's detail. The word scar is also a designation for patterns that are indiscernible. In some cases, a scar pattern
will arbitrarily take the pattern of the finger in the opposite hand.

The detail of the friction skin also contains ridge characteristics.
These characteristics are also known as points, points of identification, or minutia. Characteristics are deviations in the continuity of a
friction ridge. These characteristics are often expressed in, but not
limited to, the following common friction skin characteristics.

B. Common Friction Skin Characteristics

(Characteristics are also known as points of identification or minutia.)

A. *Ending ridge.*

B. *Bifurcation* (Dividing ridge).

C. *Dot* (Extremely short ridge being as long as it is wide).

D. *Enclosure* or *Lake* (Two close and connected bifurcations).

E. *Trifurcation* (A true trifurcation would be one ridge dividing into three, yet most all examples are actually two very close and connected bifurcations that share one ridge).

F. *Short ridge* or *Island* (Two ending ridges connected by a very short ridge).

G. *Right angle intersection* (Separate ridge intersection common in cores of loops, tented arches, and palmar thenar areas. Some right angle intersections are called ridge connections or crossings. Also, some types of crossings may actually be forms of bifurcations.).

H. *Bridge* (Connected bifurcations sharing one ridge).

I. *Spur* (Combination of short ridge and bifurcation).

J. *Triradius* (An intersection of separate ridges often found in the delta areas. A triradius is similar in appearance to a bifurcation yet, with a greater angle between the separate ridge intersections).

However, these ten listed characteristics can be considered as mostly combinations originating from just two characteristics, the bifurcation and the ending ridge. The dot is considered by some fingerprint specialists as the ultimate in a short ridge. The dot can also be included with the ending ridge and bifurcation as one of the basic characteristic types from which other characteristics and characteristic groups are made. The additional characteristics D-J can be considered as combinations of the basic ridge ending and bifurcation.

In making a fingerprint identification, all characteristics present are considered, whether they are in single or group form. While the highest percentage of fingerprint characteristics are the ending ridges and bifurcations, the presence of such in group form may make the fingerprint impression's arrangement more uncommon.[4] Also considered would be a print impression's clarity and degree of distortion. Some automated fingerprint identification computer systems (AFIS) break the fingerprint information down to these basic levels of ending ridges and bifurcations. With these types of systems, a search is based upon a combination of information, including the fingerprint pattern type, core placement within the pattern, and the spatial relationships of the characteristics (see Fig. 6). The search computer organizes the fingerprint's characteristic information mathematically via a mathematical algorithm. The fingerprint's pattern type designation sets the computer search parameter, thus limiting the scope of the search to only like pattern types (see also Chapter 11).

The uniqueness of certain arrangements of characteristics is, of course, partly based on their rarity and shape. In regard to statistical averages for availability of characteristics, the most probable would be ending ridges, followed by bifurcations. The remaining characteristics and/or characteristic groupings would have much lower probabilities. In areas of friction ridges that contain no such characteristics,

---

4. It should also be noted that the lack of characteristics in a specified area is just as important as the inclusion of a characteristic

just continuous ridges, this too would be a factor in considering the spatial relationships of the characteristics themselves (Cowger, 1983, p. 145). Comparisons of fingerprints for identification rely on the correct spatial relationships of characteristics, as well as the lack of characteristics.

It is a well-known fact that ending ridges and bifurcations are sometimes indistinguishable from one another when comparing multiple impressions of the same fingerprint. Various factors can affect the impression process, such as pressure, surface contamination, surface texture, and distortion due to the flexibility of the skin and/or receiving surface. Incipient ridges, which are underdeveloped friction ridges that lack the sweat pores of normal friction ridges, are also subjected to variations in reproduction due to the listed factors (see also Chapter 8, section 2).

2. WHO HAS FRICTION SKIN?

Friction skin has a genetic foundation that determines its overall structure in addition to the identification possibilities of its details. Friction skin has been found on humans, primates, and a similar version on the marsupial koala.[5] Friction skin has even been found on the gripping side of the tail of a red howler monkey (Berry, 1991). While it has been observed that the shape and structure of the friction skin are similar between these animals, only minor research has been done on its genetic foundations and its availability.

Another interesting comparison of friction ridge skin occurs in human identical twins. Identical (monozygotic) twins are identical because they originate from the same ova. These twins will often share similar fingerprint patterns and shapes, yet the spatial relationships of the friction skin's finely detailed characteristics still vary. It seems that our human nature tends to let us lump together things that are similar on a macroscopic level, while ignoring smaller details outside our immediate vision. This is also reflected in how we structure our written and verbal sentences. Thus, the term *identical twins* is essentially a generality, because most people are not referring to the fact that twins originated from an identical embryonic zygote or ova.

---

5. Friction skin used for gripping on animals outside the primates immediate ancestry seems to be a case of convergent evolution.

Yet, most people are aware that identical twins do not look identical at all, just very similar. The point here is to illustrate that fingerprint identifications are not based on similar fingerprints, only fingerprints from an identical source. This identical source would be from one area of friction skin.

The only remaining question from a fingerprint identification perspective is would cloned primates have sufficiently similar friction ridge characteristics that would affect a standard fingerprint type identification? This is a question that many in the identification field would like to know. To date, there has not been a true cloning of a primate, let alone of the Homo sapiens version. Genetic mutations are introduced into the genetic replication process with a certain average frequency. These mutations ensure genetic variability and uniqueness. The real question may then be, would the frequency of mutation introductions be enough to maintain sufficiently different friction ridge characteristics between cloned pairs? Well, if identical twins are any clue, the answer would be yes.

3. INFANT FOOTPRINTING

Identification is the sole reason for footprinting newborn babies. The friction ridge detail that contains the identifying characteristics is easier to obtain from the feet of newborn infants. This is due to the infant's foot having less articulating capabilities and more distinctive detail than does the hand.[6] Infant footprints can prove to be of great value when identification of the child comes into question. The likelihood that an inked fingerprint card would be available for a child is remote.

Unfortunately, many hospital personnel are unaware that footprinting is simply a means of identification and should be done before the infant is separated from its mother. It is very common to find that infant footprint impressions that are of such poor quality that they are of no identification value. The original footprint records that are microfilmed may be of no identification value even when printed for viewing. Many hospitals no longer provide a footprinting service due to a variety of reasons. Unfortunately, some of the hospitals that still

---

6. Infant hands are so small and delicate that it is simply much easier to make friction skin impressions from the foot's sole (plantar) surface.

do provide the service use a timesaving pre inked plastic screen that proves near useless for reproducing identifiable friction skin characteristic detail.

Some of the Problems Encountered with Footprint Comparisons

- No footprint impressions were made at time of birth.
- Pre inked transfer screen did not reproduce details and characteristics of the footprint.
- Footprint impressions were smudged or smeared.
- Hospital staff adding unreproduced detail such as toes with pencil eraser or similar instrument.
- Some footprint impressions are kept in hospital records for only a few years.
- All birth papers, including footprints, are microfilmed and originals are destroyed. Microfilm is often insufficient to reproduce the details of an original footprint.

It is not unheard of for an adult to have his or her original birth footprint impressions compared to current impressions of their foot for verification of birth records. The fingerprint specialist may make a photographic enlargement of the infant footprint to minimize the size difference for ease of comparison. A good quality infant footprint impression can be of great value in cases of infants being switched, orphaned, kidnapped, or in cases of an accident. The soles of the feet are often protected from serious damage by footwear during fire, or airplane and automobile accidents (see Fig. 3).

Chapter 3

FRICTION SKIN CLASSIFICATION

1. FINGERPRINT CLASSIFICATION SCHEMES

W hile identification with friction ridge characteristics is the means to verify a person's identity, there also exists a need to organize all the fingerprint information into a usable and practical filing system. Even a small fingerprint database would quickly prove useless without some scheme for retrieval of similar fingerprints. This need for an efficient system was quickly realized by the pioneers in fingerprint science. The 10-print fingerprint card is the classified document that would be filed (see Fig. 20).

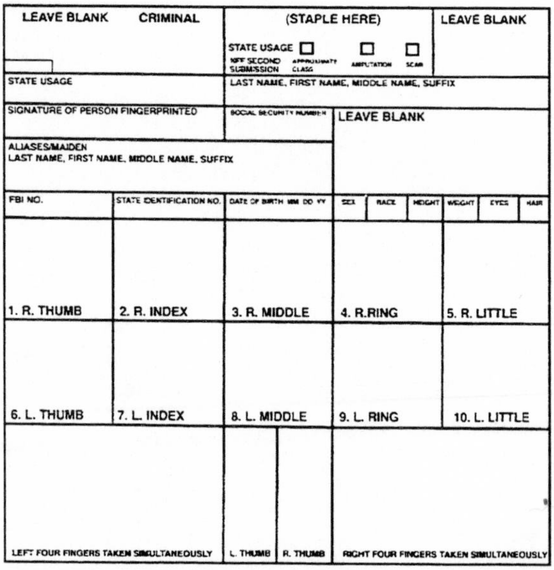

Figure 20. Standardized criminal format 10-print card.

24

There are three major types of classification systems in use today. The first is the century–old Henry classification system. This system is a manual file system that uses the fingerprint pattern types overviewed in Chapter 2, section A. The Henry system allows 10-print cards to be evaluated and analyzed using a pattern classification formula. The fingerprint card can then be filed according to specific rules of this formula. The original version of the Henry system was designed to file fingerprint cards in boxes on a wall. This wall file would consist of rows of boxes, 32 long by 32 boxes high. The classification formula, calculated from all 10 fingers, would qualify the 10-print card to be stored in one of the 1024 boxes. Other information in the formula would provide information for what sequence within the box the fingerprint card belonged. Future 10-print cards could be analyzed with this same classification formula and compared to file prints that would have a similar classification. The system was proven successful as identical an identical fingerprint card could now be located easily from an extensive collection of cards.

An example of the Henry classification formula layout.

Right hand	<u>14 O 19 W OOO 14</u>
Left hand	L 2 U OMI

This type of system has been fine-tuned over the years to accommodate the millions of cards in some file systems. The Henry system is a manual labor process that is inefficient on larger scales. The basic formula of a fingerprint classification system is derived from analyzing finger position, pattern types, ridge counts in specific areas of the pattern, and the ridge flow within the pattern. The breakdown of this classification system is a book in itself and cannot be detailed here. However, the FBI's *Science of Fingerprints* details fingerprint pattern classification, the Henry classification formula, and its filing system protocol.

The second type of classification system is the NCIC system or National Crime Information Center Fingerprint Classification System. Of course, you do not need be a criminal to have your fingerprints classified with this system. The NCIC system is not intended for filing of fingerprint cards like the Henry system. With modern computer information systems, a database was needed that details information about the fingerprints *themselves*, not just where to find them in some file. Thus, the NCIC system describes what the individual fingerprint impressions look like. This system is an evaluation process based on many Henry system classification rules. The 20-digit NCIC code for describing each finger is displayed as two code positions for each finger. The code, or a classification, starts with the right thumb and counts sequentially with the left thumb occupying the 11th and 12th digits in the code string. The last two digits of code are assigned to the left little finger (see Fig. 21). Loop-type patterns are assigned a number, while arches and whorls are assigned letters. The two-digit designation for whorl patterns starts with the letter of the pattern, such as (D) for double loop and ends with the first letter of the tracing as outlined by Henry Classification rules. Thus (DO) would be a double-loop whorl with an outer-type tracing. An (XM) would be an accidental whorl with a (meet) tracing. Ridge tracing is simply a description of how certain ridges are arranged relative to each other.

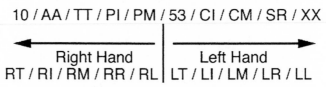

Figure 21. NCIC Classification.

In the example Figure 21, the first number 10 is the right thumb and the number 53 is the left thumb. Each number or letter combination gives the information of pattern type, and for loops, the ridge count between the delta and the core is represented by the actual number found in the code boxes. Reference Figure 6 for core and delta information. Ridge counts of 1-49 are for ulnar loops, and ridge counts for radial loops start at 51. In our example, the right thumb is an ulnar loop with a ridge count of 10 and the left thumb is a radial loop with a ridge count of 3. AA is for plain arch, and TT is for tented arch. Whorls are also represented with two-letter codes according to standard Henry classification rules. The designation of (SR) is for scar. SR is used where the fingerprint pattern cannot be clearly deciphered due to scaring, injury, or excessive wear. XX is the designation for amputation. Here, the fingerprint specialist would know to look for partial or total amputation of the left little finger. If we have this information available, along with a current fingerprint card of interest, we would be able to ascertain if the fingerprints are similar enough to warrant contacting a fingerprint specialist for closer inspection or comparison. Also, if the patterns differ substantially, then it could be assumed that these two records are for two different persons.

Some drawbacks to the computerized NCIC fingerprint classification system is the fact that it may not always be correct. Input errors may cause identifications to go unnoticed. Also, once errors are discovered, they are not always corrected for various bureaucratic reasons. Another reason is simply a limitation of the classification system. Like the Henry, system the NCIC is intended for use in referencing all ten fingers as they are found on a 10-print card. The system specifies between ulnar and radial loops. When making a distinction between ulnar and radial loops, it must be known from which hand the fingerprint impression originated. If the print is out of context, such as a crime scene print, it is not possible to classify loop patterns with an ulnar or radial designation. Whether the system being used is NCIC or Henry, out-of-context loop patterns are simply described as a left or right slant loop of a particular ridge count.

It is not possible to classify into a formula any individual fingerprint pattern types because it would probably not be known from which hand a fingerprint originated. However, *it is possible* for more than one person to have the same classification for any of the classification schemes. Matching fingerprint classifications simply means that further comparisons of individual characteristics are needed.

The third major classification system is the numerical system. A numerical system is a number-based system that is used in conjunction with AFIS (automated fingerprint identification system) computers. Much of the original Henry classified fingerprint files have been converted to computerized numerical file systems. Once an AFIS fingerprint file is entered using some very simplified or modified Henry classification rules the file is assigned a permanent unique number or alpha-numeric code such as #NV123456.

By design, a computer does not need to search the entire database of fingerprints if any of the search patterns are known. If one or more patterns are known at the time of search, the computer needs to search only like pattern types. (For more information, see Chapter 11 on AFIS classification and computer database fingerprint searches.)

A fingerprint's pattern type is used for classification. Classifications are used for the sorting of individual fingerprints and/or fingerprint cards. A classification is not fingerprint identification and cannot be used for identification.

As classification systems are fine-tuned or made obsolete by technology, older terminology may no longer be used (see also Appendix A). Efforts have been made in the identification field to simplify terminology. Medical terms are used in some instances, yet layman's terms are better understood by investigators and juries.

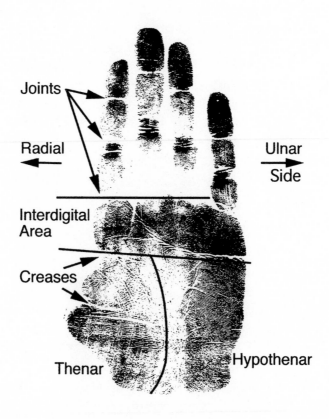

Figure 22. Major palmar characteristics.

2. PALM PRINT/FOOTPRINT CLASSIFICATION

The large-scale classification of palmprint impressions for data entry or archival filing is a relatively new concept. Only recently has the technology been available to enter palmprints into computer databases. Ordinarily, palmprints are simply filed along with the 10-print card of the individual as most AFIS computer databases allow only searches of fingerprints. Fingerprint impressions made from the last joint on each finger are recorded onto 10-print cards. These 10-print cards are the standard fingerprint identification medium. Palmprints that do not include fingers are generally not used in routine identification. However, palmprints are used often when comparing crime scene print impressions.

The soles of the feet also bear friction skin complete with identifiable characteristics, yet only a few footprint files exist. These few files are all noncomputerized-type files of inked foot impressions. Impressions of the toes offer pattern types similar to fingerprints. Yet, the complete inking of individual toes for impressions used in identification is not feasible. However, the ball area of the foot does offer a large pad that easily reproduces highly detailed print impressions. This ball area is where footprints are classified. The FBI does have a footprint classification system and maintains a limited use file. This file is mainly used for persons with no hands or fingers.

Footprints are also of value in cases of fire or accident, as footwear often protects the friction skin on the feet from serious damage. The military is a primary user of footprint files. However, modern methods of DNA replication have, mostly, succeeded in replacing footprint identification when no fingerprints are available. (See Figures 2, 3, and 22 for samples of palm and footprint impressions.)

Chapter 4

EXEMPLAR FINGERPRINT IMPRESSIONS

1. INKED FINGERPRINTS

What is an inked fingerprint? This question is a very important part of understanding how most fingerprint identifications are made, and how fingerprint files and databases are created. Essentially, an inked fingerprint is an impression of friction skin made with a medium such as printer's ink. Ink is applied to the top surface of the friction ridges on the last joint of the finger, the entire palmar surface, or soles of the feet. These inked fingerprints can also be known as exemplar prints. Exemplar prints are intentionally recorded friction skin impressions from a known person.[1] Again, the term fingerprint is an all encompassing term and could be in reference to any area of the palmar surface or even soles of the feet which are called the plantar surfaces.

The term inked, as in inked fingerprint, is also a generality. A black printer type of ink has long been the standard medium used for recording friction ridge skin impressions. However, it is not the only means of making an exemplar impression. A computer-generated fingerprint image, often termed *live-scan*, offers a considerable speed advantage when compared to standard ink-type methods. It is common to record up to four fingerprint documents of an individual at a single printing event.[2] Live-scan-type fingerprint imaging systems are

---

1. Exemplar prints are those prints from a known origin or source. However, the person's true identity may not always be known without further investigation.
2. Three of the documents may consist of duplicate 10-print cards destined for comparison and filing with local, state, and national government agencies. The court system may also receive documents with inked fingerprints.

30

used to electronically scan fingerprints. These images can then be printed to 10-print cards via a computer laser printer. Current laser printer systems used for fingerprint reproduction print in the range of 300 to 500 dpi resolution. With live-scan, the fingerprint scanning process is done only once, and duplicate 10-print cards can be printed as needed. Live-scan systems are fast–becoming the system of choice at larger agencies. (See also Appendix C and section 2 of this chapter.)

Another form of inked fingerprints, albeit nonstandard, may include elimination fingerprints in the form of purposely made and developed latent print impressions. This is an alternate method of recording victim elimination fingerprints when ink is not available. Field officers or a fingerprint specialist will have subjects press their fingers onto a white card stock. This transfers oils and moisture residues from the fingers to the blank card. Then a contrasting color of fingerprint development powder is applied to the card to develop the fingerprints. The card is then labeled with basic case and finger–print information. Clear tape is applied over the impressions to prevent smearing of the delicate residues. This system works because the powdering is done immediately after the impressions are made. The moisture and oils contained in the fingerprint residues have not had time to evaporate or soak into the card stock. Properly made elimination prints of this type can offer quality similar to regular inked fingerprints. These elimination prints can then be used in comparisons just as inked fingerprints would, although, here the fingerprint record would not be durable enough to withstand entry into a file system and is almost always filed with the latent fingerprint evidence.

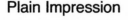

Plain Impression   **Rolled Impression**

Figure 23. Two types of inked fingerprint impressions.

Major case prints, or major criminal prints, are recorded impressions that represent all areas of friction skin on the palmar, and if necessary, plantar surface of the feet. Major case prints are recorded in addition to the standardized 10-print and palmprint cards. The very tips of the fingers, sides of the fingers, and sides of the palms are not always represented in normal printing of fingers and palms. Recovered crime-sceneprint impressions may be from one of these areas; thus, major case prints are needed before a comparison can take place. All fingerprint impressions represent only a fragment of a whole. Here, a whole print would be the three–dimensional palmar surface of a hand. Generally, most all ink and developed latent print impressions are two-dimensional fragments of a particular sample of friction skin. Major case prints are a collection of overlapping areas of inked friction skin impressions (see Fig. 24). The only way to record a *complete* palm impression is to make a three-dimensional mold of the palmar surface. The same is true regarding just the last joint of each finger; the patterned area of a finger, it is still not possible to record a complete impression at one time using standard inking practices. Even if the finger is rolled from one side to the other, the tip of the finger will not be represented because our receiving medium, a 10-print card, is a two-dimensional object.

Finger Tips   Rolled Finger   Rolled Finger Tip

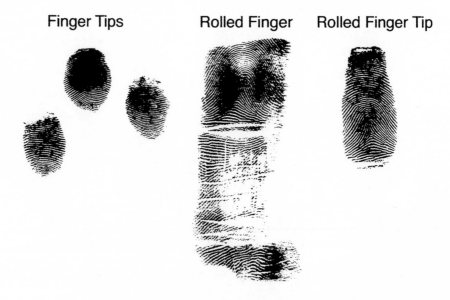

Figure 24. Major-case type fingerprint impressions.

In a detailed report of a comparison of inked fingerprints, one would expect precision in describing the exact area or areas that were compared. An example would be: Inked fingerprint card from John Doe was compared with known prints of Christopher Clyde Jones ID#123456 with date of birth 01-12-1975. A subsequent conclusion of *identification* or *no identification* would follow. Exacting descriptors allows the prints in question to be verified and/or inspected by involved parties.

Clerical errors can occasionally be made that allow inaccurate information, in all or part, to accompanying the inked fingerprints. 10-print fingerprint cards contain areas of information that are intended to be filled out at time of printing (see Fig. 1). Name, date of birth, date of printing, addresses, name of printer, and the fingerprints themselves each need to be accurately recorded.

2. LIVE-SCAN TECHNOLOGY

Live-scan is the computerized equivalent of inked fingerprints. A person's fingerprints are scanned via a glass mirror reflection and electronic camera, or by such new technology as ferroelectric infrared thermal imaging.[3] The information from the fingerprint scans are converted into a digital computer code. Once the 10 fingerprint images are captured, the user can print out duplicate 10-print fingerprint cards on a high-resolution laser printer (see also Appendix C). Current live-scan technology resides at 300-500 dpi image resolution.[4] A 500 dpi is sufficient to reproduce some of the pores that line the tops of the frictions ridges. The lower 300 dpi systems cannot reproduce the pore or ridge edge detail reliably, yet it is sufficient for basic fingerprint identification when the live-scan machines are properly maintained and operated. (See Appendix C for a comparison of a computer generated live-scan and an inked fingerprint.)

---

3. There are several different imaging solutions available. With the exception of the reflection mirror live-scan, most of the technology is relatively new and nonstandardized. The ferroelectric infrared thermal contrast system is being developed by the Thomson-CSF company (McCarthy, 1999).

4. The abbreviation of "dpi" is for dots per inch. Not all electronic images, or image output, are defined in dot per inch resolutions. Thus, printed resolutions may vary. Dye sublimation printers, for example, print in "ppi" or pixels per inch. Also, the capture resolution of a fingerprint image also affects the output resolution.

A live-scan generated 10-print card is similar in appearance to a regular inked card. The differences may include the addition of computer code added to the margin of the card. A gray scale bar and a laser printed operator's name in lieu of a signature may also be present. Since all machines require a user specific password to access the imaging program, this has not proven to be a problem. This lack of hand written data also increases the accuracy of the data itself by not breaking the electronic chain of combining the fingerprint image data and the personal data during the printing process. Of course, agencies will have to supervise the use of the machine to ensure that other operators do not use the same passwords and log-on name.

In large agencies, live-scan electronic images are slowly replacing ink as the primary means of creating a fingerprint record. While ink requires that each finger is inked prior to each impression, live-scan allows each finger to be scanned as repeatedly as necessary to generate a clear fingerprint impression, but the best detailed image need only be captured once.[5]

In general, novice, live-scan, computerized systems operators can produce clearer *overall* impressions when compared to using ink. Clearer images are the result of the fact that a live-scan operator has no reason to accept and capture a smudged image.[6] The print can be rerolled until a satisfactory image has been made. Once this is achieved, the operator will move on to the next finger until all 10 fingers are rolled on the glass platen, then the plain impressions of each four fingers and thumbs are made along the lower part of the 10-print card. These nonrolled plain impressions will help ensure that the 10 fingers were rolled correctly (see Fig. 1). This procedure has not changed from the ink process. The fact that it is much easier to reroll fingers with the live-scan systems seems to generate better overall impressions with novice operators as well. Clearer 10-print cards equal a better database and an improved match, or hit rate, on subsequent database searches.

---

5. The term capture of a fingerprint is that the image is digitally acquired for further processing and subsequent printing.

6. While live-scan type print impressions generally result in a clearer overall fingerprint impression database, most fingerprint specialists prefer properly made ink impressions for comparison purposes. Ink allows great detail, if properly done. The problem results from the fact that unsupervised and/or undertrained fingerprint technicians in jail booking areas or public fingerprint counters will often produce a higher percentage of smudged fingerprints using the ink method.

The disadvantages of the live-scan systems are that most are not portable and require high maintenance. The systems and printers must be calibrated often to produce quality fingerprint impressions. Computer-generated artifacts can also be added to a fingerprint impression by the operator, the system software, or by the computer printer. User errors can result in the fingerprint of one individual being added to the information and name of another. These instances are rare they are not unique to live-scan hardware as they can also be found with the traditional ink method. One of the main reasons for errors with computer-based systems may be because the operator may not always know what data the computer is currently processing. A 10-print card could be fed into a printer which is printing a different individual's fingerprints. Most systems attempt to avoid this problem by eliminating as much handwritten data as possible by keeping the alpha-numeric data and the fingerprint images together throughout the printing process. A similar problem was noted with standard inked 10-print cards. If the descriptor data, such as name and date of birth, was not added to the fingerprint cards immediately after the printing of a person, it was possible that the wrong information could be added. With current systems, the main problems reside with the reprinting of data from electronic storage buffers, or the printing of miscellaneous 10-print cards that are provided by the customers.

The most notorious drawback of computer-generated fingerprints is not from the occasional error but an inability to reproduce very fine fingerprint detail. Computer-generated images often lack the *nuances* of a rolled ink fingerprint. These fine details or nuances are often used to compare fingerprints. So the trade-off seems to be that while computer-generated fingerprint images save time and can enhance the computer database's hit ratio, they can also prove difficult for use in some of the more challenging fingerprint comparisons. The comparison of crime scene latent fingerprint impressions often rely on the fine fingerprint ridge detail.

Generally, exemplar and latent fingerprint impression quality is highly variable. As was mentioned earlier, it is not that uncommon to see crime scene latent fingerprints that are of a higher quality than the exemplar prints on file. Whether the exemplar fingerprint impressions are ink or computer-generated, the actual quality and detail of the print will determine its usefulness in comparisons.

Chapter 5

LATENT FINGERPRINT DEVELOPMENT AND RECOVERY

1. LATENT FINGERPRINTS

What are latent fingerprints? Latent fingerprints are friction skin impressions made of moisture, eccrine gland secretions, transferred sebaceous oils, or other substances that are of such low contrast relative background that they are generally not visible to the unaided eye[1](see Figs. 4 & 25). These latent fingerprint impressions can actually be made from most any substance. The difference is that latent impressions are most always made unintentionally, and are often of extremely low contrast when compared with regular inked exemplar fingerprints.[2] As with inked fingerprints, the term latent fingerprint is a generality that is used to describe a nonink impression left by any friction ridge skin. Specifically, the word *latent* is that which is in a nonvisible state or hidden from view. The opposite is *patent* fingerprints. Patent fingerprints are fingerprints that are visible under normal viewing conditions.[3] However, most all crime scene fingerprint impressions are commonly called latent prints. Even latent print impressions, which may be visible to the unaided eye are often oxymoronically termed visible latent fingerprint impressions. These low contrast latent fingerprint impressions would need to be contrast enhanced to make them visible to the human eye.

1. Aside from water and oils, pore residues can consist of lipids, amino acid, proteins, salts, and other chemicals contained within the body.
2. Inked fingerprints are generally intentionally made exemplar prints of known persons.
3. Latent, to be hidden, and patent, to be visible, are words of Latin origin.

Electromagnetic Spectrum (Not to scale)

Gamma–X rays–Ultra–violet–(visible)–Infrared–Microwave–TV
–Radio
Visible = (violet, blue, green, yellow, orange, red)
Visible light combined = white light.

The latent fingerprint development range includes long wavelength Ultraviolet (UV or black light) through the visible colors including red.

There is, of course, more descriptive terminology that is used when the details of a fingerprint impression need to be known. For instance, the statement fingerprints were found at the scene of a crime, may be all the information needed at that period of the investigation. Yet, eventually, we may need to know all the information that is available. Thus, a more descriptive statement of the facts may be; a latent fingerprint developed on the side surface of a drinking glass was found on the kitchen table of listed address. In essence, contrast-enhancing processes and techniques enable the latent print to be separated from its background so it could be documented and recovered as evidence. Subsequently, comparisons with known exemplar fingerprints can be made.

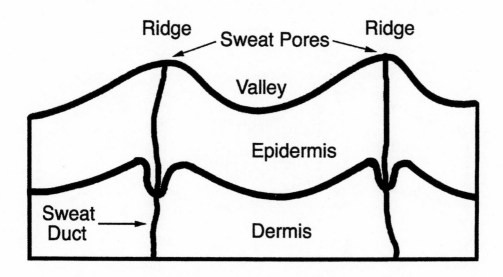

Figure 25. Cross section of friction skin.

The content of the latent print impression is usually the oils and moisture residues that are transferred from the friction skin ridges to the surface, or negative impressions where surface residues have been removed by the friction skin(see Figs. 25 & 26). When an object is handled or contacted in some manner by friction ridges, the pressure applied to the contact area may result in a transfer of materials in one or both directions. A negative fingerprint impression caused by the removal of residues from a surface is called a reversal (see also Chapter 8, section 3). Multiple print impressions are two, or more impressions from an identical source. Each print in a multiple print series will vary in quality and reproduced detail. A single impression can be a well-detailed reproduction of the friction skin complete with identifying characteristics, or it can simply be a smudge mark that may not even be identifiable as having been made by friction skin. The concept is similar to a rubber stamp: The proper amount of ink (residue) and a smooth even pressure will leave an impression (touch) that is a detailed reproduction of the stamp's surface. Too much ink and uneven pressure on the stamp will leave a less than worthy reproduction that may not be readable. Latent fingerprints, as well as inked fingerprints, reproduce in this manner. A fingerprint specialist will examine and possibly compare, developed fingerprints in varying degrees of clarity. Figure 50 shows the volar pad areas of the palm that are commonly found as latent print impressions.

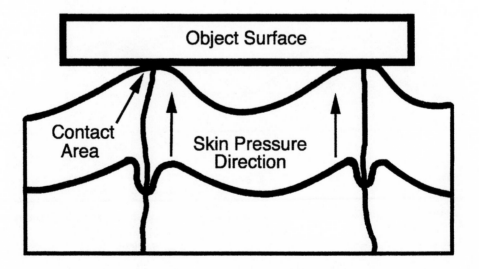

Figure 26. Surface contact and residue transfer areas.

A patent print or visible latent impression is often found in soft pliable surfaces such as putty, grease, or dust. These soft surfaces will often yield high definition impressions; however, low contrast situations may even render these impressions as true latent prints. Strong oblique lighting will often enhance the contrast of these types of impressions. This is similar in the manner in which shoe and tire tracks are prepared for photography.

A surface's porosity, texture, and composition will affect how well any fingerprint residues will be transferred, as well as how detailed the impression will be.[4] These concepts are readily apparent when a single latent print impression covers multiple surfaces. On a surface, such as a bottle with a label, it is common to note that the detail in a developed fingerprint impression will abruptly stop at the glass-label border. Either surface may have a detailed impression while the adjacent surface lacks all or part of the impression (see Fig. 27). Hard, smooth, nonporous surfaces are ideal for developing latent print impressions. This means that hard, smooth, nonporous surfaces are ideal for receiving latent print impressions.

The fact that friction skin is semipliable, contains various degrees of residues, and can be applied with varying pressures to different surfaces means the development of latent print impressions can be measured using the science of statistics. Statistics must be used since it is not possible to determine exact conditions for fingerprint deposition, nor is it always possible to find, develop, and document all latent fingerprint impressions that may be present on a surface. These statistics are often based on simple research of recovery rates of identifiable fingerprints recovered from a particular sample. An example may be of 100 aluminum 12 oz. beverage cans processed for latent fingerprint impressions, identifiable latent fingerprints were developed on 20 cans. Thus, 20% of the cans yielded identifiable latent fingerprints. Of these cans, it could be further averaged for how many identifiable fingerprints were found per can. While it is uncommon for the fingerprint specialist to keep detailed statistical information, it may be useful when evaluating a new development process or when comparing processes and techniques currently in use.

---

4. The word "composition" is in reference to a surface's material construction or substrate, as well as, any surface residues that may be present.

With latent fingerprint impressions that are deposited onto hard nonporous surfaces, it is found that the water-based moisture components of the latent print residues will tend to evaporate rather quickly. In comparison, any oils in the fingerprint residue will tend to last considerably longer.[5]   For both porous and nonporous surfaces, the oil residues of a latent fingerprint can often survive minor contact with water intact.

On some metal surfaces, these slowly evaporating oils may etch a durable impression. Generally, an etched impression is an indication that significant time has passed allowing a rather slow chemical process to take place. Of course, there are numerous factors involved that prevent assigning a date to the application of the latent impression (see also Chapter 7). Since there are numerous variables involved in the creation of a latent print; there is always a good chance that a latent print; of sufficient definition would not be transferred to an object. Also, there exists the possibility that current latent print development technology is insufficient to develop all latent print impressions that may be present on a given object.[6]

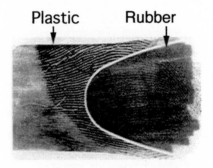

Figure 27. Latent print over two surface types.

---

5. Temperature will also greatly affect evaporation rates.
6. It is also a possibility that the receiving surface did not readily accept a latent print impression. Residues may not have adhered to the surface.

2. POWDER DEVELOPMENT OF LATENT FINGERPRINT IMPRESSIONS

Contrast is the key to development of latent print impressions. Whether the development of the latent print is by a fine powder substance, chemical reaction, or by an alternate light source (forensic light), the result is the same. Contrast is increased between the latent print impression and the background on which it resides. Black fingerprint powder has long been the staple development medium for latent prints. Development powders consist of a very fine grain substance that varies in formula depending on manufacturer and powder color. Powders adhere to the oils and moistures that make up a latent print. It is thought that temperature plays a role in how effective a powder can be. In warmer temperatures, the oils in many fingerprint residues are in a soft state. It is thought that powders may adhere better to softer residues. The wide variety of colored powders available allows the user to apply a color that contrasts with the prints background to better visualize any impressions. Some colored powders are designed for use with lasers and alternate light sources (see also Chapter 6).

Powders are applied with a soft fiber brush. The most common is a brush made of fiberglass attached to a small straight handle. The development powders are loaded into the brush by dipping the brush into a supply of powder. The brush is then gently wiped, brushed, or spun over the surface suspected as having latent fingerprint impressions. The soft powder-laden fibers will transfer powder to the latent print residues. The brushing action can continue until sufficient contrast has been achieved or the print's detail starts to degrade due to the brushing action. The developed latent print impression is then photographed and/or lifted using a special transparent adhesive tape or a sticky rubber lifter. When removed from the surface, the developed latent print can be transferred to a lift card and protected for long-term preservation as evidence. (See also "Recovering Developed Latent Fingerprint Impressions" in this chapter.)

Latent fingerprints developed with dark powders are usually lifted with transparent tape and preserved on white card stock called lift cards. Black powder can even be used on dark colored surfaces. With a strong oblique light source, the reflective difference between the black powder and its background is usually sufficient to visualize any developed fingerprint impressions. Many colored powders are usually photographed with contrast enhancing photographic filters and/or in conjunction with an alternate light source prior to attempting fingerprint recovery. Many powders are actually designed to fluoresce under specific light energies (see also Chapter 6, section 2).

Magnetic powders are also very successful in developing latent print impressions. Magnetic powders consist of iron filings of various sizes. A magnetic applicator (magnetic brush) is used to apply the metal-based powder over the surface of an object. As the magnetic powder is wiped over the surface, the ultra small particles suspended in the larger iron filings adhere to the oils and moisture of the latent print residues.[7] A moist layer of human breath applied (condensed) onto a latent print prior to or during the application of the magnetic powder is a popular enhancement method. The moisture and warmth in the breath soften the oils in the latent residue. Much of the breath's moisture will quickly evaporate while the oils will remain soft for a sufficient time to be developed. Once a print is adequately developed, it is photographed and/or lifted for preservation in the same manner as with regular powder. This preservation is discussed in the next section of this chapter. Magnetic powder may work on surfaces where regular powders are not effective. What these surfaces are will depend on the surface in question, and the environmental factors that have influenced the latent print residues. The process of deciding which development powder type and color to use is often based on experience and experimentation.

Over time, the very small development particles are depleted and the magnetic powder looses much of its effectiveness. Magnetic powder should be periodically replaced when it fails to leave a distinct powder trail when wiped (brushed) over a surface. Regular nonmagnetic black, gray, and colored powders do not lose their effectiveness over time and can be used until the powder supply is depleted or becomes contaminated with hazardous substances such as blood and drug residues.

Like regular development powders, magnetic powders come in various colors. Some of these colors have fluorescing capabilities with special light sources. Regardless of the type of development process used, the developed latent prints must be seen by the human

7. Magnetic powders and regular powders will also adhere to other moistures and oils present on the surface in question.

factor to be preserved as evidence. Thus, processing should not be undertaken without a strong light source such as a flashlight or desk lamps to aid in the visualizing of any low contrast developed latent prints.

The application of magnetic powders to ferrousmagnetic metals is not often recommended, yet it is sometimes effective. Usually, the excess powder fails to drop off the metal surface due to magnetism. The inherent magnetism of the metal also prevents all excess powder from being retrieved by the magnetic brush. Compressed air or human breath is best to clear the extra magnetic powder from the area around a developed latent print.

Extreme care should be used when processing electronic items such as credit cards with magnetic strips, magnetic storage mediums, or other magnetic hardware. Magnetic powder within electronic and electrical equipment may attract to electrically charged surfaces such as disk drive heads and magnets. This may result in hardware and/or software damage. If possible, it is best to copy any magnetically stored information prior to processing.

3. RECOVERING DEVELOPED LATENT FINGERPRINT IMPRESSIONS

The preservation of developed latent fingerprint impressions enables the print to be compared with other known prints with an ultimate goal of identification. The identification of a fingerprint's source is the only reason for seeking crime scene latent fingerprints.

The main preservation techniques of developed latent fingerprints are *photography* and lifting. Photography is the reproduction of latent fingerprint impressions without physically contacting the prints themselves. Colored photographic filters are frequently used to enhance the contrast of the latent fingerprint against its background (see also Chapter 10). Lifting is the transfer of the latent residue and development medium, such as powders, to an adhesive surface such as transparent tape, or an opaque, sticky rubber pad.[8] When the tape is applied to a thin cardboard-like lift card, the impression is viewed through the tape's transparent substrate. This is the correct orientation to view developed impressions. Rubber lifters are opaque, and the resulting view of the print is backwards. Usually, the lift is then photographed and the negative is printed backwards, or the lift can be digitally acquired and the image is then flipped using imaging software for correct viewing.

When a latent print is developed with regular or magnetic powders, and is then lifted for preservation, the lifting process does not always remove all the latent residues. Sometimes the latent print can be developed more that once, or until its residues are depleted by the lifting method. These are called multiple lifts. Multiple lifts are sequential lifts of the same (identical) latent print. Once depleted, there would be insufficient latent print residue to bond with the development powders. Multiple lifts are generally only attempted if the first lift was not of clear detail. Latent fingerprints with thick residue and/or slightly smeared are good candidates for the multiple-lift technique. The first print lift may sometimes lift the smeared residues obscuring a detailed latent impression. The latent print must be repowdered each time a lift is attempted. As each lift is made, it is usually numbered in a sequence such as 1 of 3, 2/3, 3/3 etc. Once the details of the redeveloped prints start to degrade, repowdering and lifting are usually stopped. The best lift of the series is then marked for use in any future comparisons.

When a lift is made and transferred to a lift card, all pertinent information for that lift should also be recorded thereat. Some of the basic information needed to make a lift of a developed latent print relevant for a case includes:

```
┌─────────────────────────────────────────────────┐
│ Case / Report #_____  Date_____        │
│ Offense Type _____  Officer_____         │
│ Location _____        │
│ Victim / Subject _____        │
│     Description and diagram of lift location:     │
│                                                   │
│                                                   │
│                                                   │
│                                                   │
│           (place lift on back of card)            │
└─────────────────────────────────────────────────┘
```

Figure 28. Sample format of latent lift card.

---

8. During the development process, the latent fingerprint residues will often absorb the development powders. Consequently, the lifting of the developed print includes the lifting of much of the fingerprint residue itself.

Basic Information for a Latent Lift Card

• A detailed description of the latent print lift location.
• The Date lift was made.
• Officer making lift.
• Address of incident.

Without most of this important information the evidentary value or relevance of the recovered latent fingerprint may be disputable. This is especially true if similar crime scenes overlap in location and/or time. To this basic information any additional details can only build a foundation to the existing value of the latent print.

Additional Information on a Lift Card May Include

• Direction indicator such as arrows for UP or for NORTH, when relevant.
• Diagram of object showing lift location.
• Indication if latent lift is one in a series of multiple lifts of the same impression.
• Indication if other lifts were made of adjacent areas.

Large developed latent print impressions, such as a palm or consecutive fingers, can be lifted in several ways. Lifting tape is available in many sizes, with 1.5, 2, and 4 inch widths being common. These tapes can be overlapped by about .25 of an inch to increase their effective lift area. If the overlapped tape (latent print area) exceeds the size of a standard lift card it is common to find the blank backside of a 8x8 inch 10-print card converted for use as a latent lift card. The backside of a 10-print card allows enough space for an entire palmprint.[9] Once the tape is overlapped on the surface and smoothed allowing the tape adhesive to bond with the developed print area, the tape is removed by lifting the bottom-most tape first while pulling all tape up as a unit. The overlapped tape lift will retain its continuity when transferred to the lift card.

Sometimes problems are encountered when attempting a lift of a latent print. One problem is that the tape adhesive will touch down

9. Not all formats of 10-print cards have a blank backside. Also, 8x8 inch cards will fit into standard 10-print type fingerprint file cabinets.

on an unintended area of the latent print or that a crease will form in the tape. These errors may obscure or obliterate part of a latent print impression. Often, when the tape contacts the latent surface in an unintentional manner, the person will attempt to salvage any part(s) of the latent print that is possible. Creased tape is often found when lifts are made from curved surfaces. A two-dimensional piece of tape being applied to a three-dimensional surface requires a special technique of rolling the adhesive side of the lift tape over the developed latent area, thus minimizing the creasing effect. The drawback is that only small areas may be lifted at a single time.

Lifting tape can often be difficult to handle, especially in cold conditions. When lifting tape is pulled from the bulk roll a negative static charge is created. This negative charge may cause the tape to attract to an object in an unexpected manner. Also, positively charged dust, dirt, and development powders may attract to the tape. This contamination of the tape is sometimes unavoidable, as it may happen when the lift of the fingerprint is being made. Often, this contamination creates bubbles in the lift that are not consistent with the background texture. While explainable, this added texture may make comparisons of the print more difficult (see also Chapter 8, section 1).

When a tape lift is made, the user will hold one or both ends of the tape and smooth the tape over the developed latent fingerprint. The ends of the tape outside the lift area are then cut or torn from the bulk roll to allow the lifted area to be transferred to the lift card. Sometimes the fingerprints of the *user* will be found on the ends of the tape. It is expected that (x's) or initials be written over known user prints to prevent any future confusion and unnecessary comparisons.

When processing a surface for latent print impressions, it is best to not attempt an evaluation of a latent print's detail while it is still on the surface of the item being processed. Normally, it is most productive to process a latent fingerprint impression to maximize its contrast, as seen against its background, then lift the print. Once lifted and applied to a white lift card, the print is free from its low contrast background and it can then be viewed with a magnifying glass to determine if it contains sufficient detail for identification purposes. The reason for lifting a fingerprint before evaluation is that sometimes high quality latent fingerprints are overlooked because they are barely visible against a low contrast, or multicolored background.

This "lift before evaluation" step is simply another contrast-enhancing method that increases the odds of finding identifiable latent fingerprints. However, on major cases, it would be wise to photograph any developed latent print impressions prior to lifting.

4. CRIME SCENE LATENT FINGERPRINT SEARCH

When a crime scene is to be searched for latent print impressions, the first step is to interview witnesses or be briefed by those that have done a preliminary investigation. Any information about what happened will let the fingerprint specialist concentrate on specific areas for the development of latent prints. If information and or evidence suggests that a suspect never came in contact with certain areas or items, there may be no need for a detailed print search in those areas. Yet, in many major crimes, crime scene technicians will often process items with even a small probability of being touched. The concept is twofold: first, the crime scene information available may be incomplete or unreliable; second, the crime scene may soon revert to public access, and this may interfere with any future evidence processing. Here, if new information is developed at some future point in the investigation, it may be impossible to return to the crime scene for any further evidence collection.

When an item or area is to be processed for latent print impressions, that surface of the area in question is evaluated for texture, material content, porosity, and dollar value. The texture, material, and porosity characteristics will determine which latent print development processes will provide the best results. An evaluation of the item's dollar value may rule out certain processes that would damage the item. Certain processes have a degree of destructive capability. For example, chemical dye stains would probably not be recommended for the interior of an automobile, except in major crime cases.

At crime scenes, large items are most often processed at the scene while small portable items are documented and collected. The items are ultimately transported to the crime lab for detailed examination and latent print processing in a controlled environment with sufficient lighting. Proper lighting is often the key to locating latent fingerprints. It is also important to remember that latent fingerprints are always fragments of a larger whole, such as a palmprint. These fragments are evaluated and compared with the aid of a 2–6 powered magnification lens.[10]   Thus, it can be reasoned that proper latent print processing will often take considerable time.

It is important to process as much of the relevant crime scene evidence as possible. To stop after developing just one, or a few, latent print impressions is counterproductive to solving crime. If any effort is warranted, then a thorough latent search is in order. The latent search is to discover who has been in contact with the evidence in question. While it is impossible to tell whether relevant fingerprints have been overlooked, if warranted, a systematic and complete search of the crime scene evidence should be within the scope of any law enforcement agency. Trained fingerprint specialists with fingerprint *identification* skills are unnecessary to complete a basic latent fingerprint search of a crime scene. Many field officers have been trained for basic crime scene fingerprint processing. However, it has been noted that a fingerprint specialist with fingerprint identification experience will, on the average, recover many more identifiable quality latent prints per crime scene.

Again, the concept of latent fingerprint development is to enhance contrast between the prints themselves and the background. If sufficient contrast can be achieved, the developed latent impression can then be preserved with photography, and/or lifting methods. Also, a developed latent print's contrast is dependent upon several factors. The angle(s) of the incident light in conjunction with the reflective and absorption characteristics of the surface affect the contrast of the developed fingerprint. The light characteristics may be such that developed fingerprint impressions may only be visible from a particular reflective angle relative to the light source. It cannot be stressed enough how important it is to have adequate ambient light available when processing with powders and chemicals. Of course, latent fingerprints will never be developed, nor recovered, if a crime scene fingerprint search is not made. Without developed latent fingerprints in which to compare, *no identifications can be made.* Without fingerprint identifications, possibly relevant crime scene *information* may go undiscovered.

---

10. Most all latent print and ink impressions are fragments. The exception would be an impression of the entire three dimensional palmar or plantar surface. Also, reference Chapter 4, Inked Fingerprints for more information.

Chapter 6

SPECIAL DEVELOPMENT PROCESSES AND CONDITIONS

1. CHEMICAL DEVELOPMENT OF LATENT FINGERPRINT IMPRESSIONS

F or most types of crime scene evidence, black and colored powders are the main development technique. Powders are
portable, easy to use, and effective on many types of surfaces. To
compliment these assorted powders are the chemical-type developers. Most processing chemicals are special as they are most effective
on particular types of surfaces. These chemicals can often be mixed
with different carriers such as solvents or other solutions. Different
solutions, such as methyl alcohol, may have different reactions with a
surface on which a latent fingerprint impression may reside. There
are also carriers called engineered fluids. These engineered fluids
can be custom designed for use with fingerprint development chemicals. They are generally safer to use and less damaging to surfaces
during their application.

The purpose of a chemical developer is to affect the latent fingerprint residues through a chemical reaction. The particular reaction is
the contrast enhancing mechanism that allows the latent fingerprint
to become visibly separated from its background. Different carrier
fluids may affect the efficiency of the particular development chemical.

On paper, cardboard, and unfinished wood surfaces, a chemical
called *ninhydrin* is very effective. Once the latent print residues soak

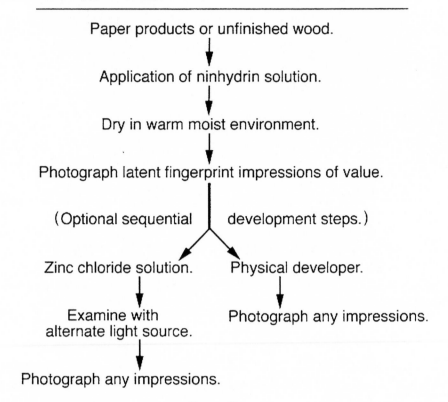

Ninhydrin application flow chart (typical).

Paper products or unfinished wood.

Application of ninhydrin solution.

Dry in warm moist environment.

Photograph latent fingerprint impressions of value.

(Optional sequential   development steps.)

Zinc chloride solution.   Physical developer.

Examine with   Photograph any impressions.
alternate light source.

Photograph any impressions.

Figure 29.

into the cellulose fibers, powder developers are no longer effective. Ninhydrin is generally applied in a liquid solution that permeates the paper fibers. This solution chemically reacts with the amino acids in the latent residues to produce a purple stain called Ruhemann's purple. The resulting ninhydrin stain result can often be enhanced, and the development process accelerated with high levels of humidity combined with the application of heat. Normally, ninhydrin-treated items are heat pressed and/or steamed with a normal household fabric iron set to medium high heat. These contrast-enhancing ninhydrin stains must be photographed within a reasonable amount of time as they may eventually fade.

Subsequent enhancement (sequential processing) of faint ninhydrin developed prints is sometimes possible using a zinc chloride (ZnCl) solution or with another process known as physical developer. Any enhanced stain is then photographed under specific lighting conditions and filtration to further increase contrast (see Fig. 29)(see also Chapter 10, section 1).

Cyanoacrylate is another popular chemical developer. Cyanoacrylate is an adhesive known as *super-glue* that was developed in the mid 1950s by Eastman Kodak. Cyanoacrylate's fingerprint development characteristics were discovered in 1978 by members of the Tokyo Metropolitan Police (Sampson, 1997 p.39). Cyanoacrylate

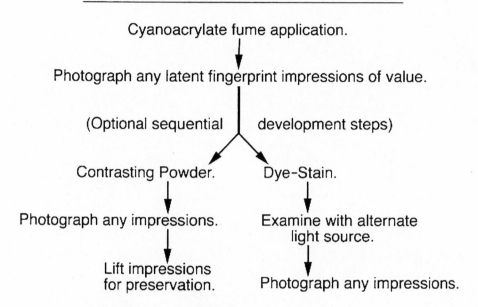

Cyanoacrylate flow chart (typical).

Cyanoacrylate fume application.

Photograph any latent fingerprint impressions of value.

(Optional sequential development steps)

Contrasting Powder.   Dye-Stain.

Photograph any impressions.   Examine with alternate light source.

Lift impressions for preservation.   Photograph any impressions.

Figure 30.

evaporates as fumes that chemically react with some of the latent print residue components. Cyanoacrylate fumed latent print impressions will take on a white, plastic appearance. The resulting developed impression is quite durable and can often be photographed as found, and/or powdered for increased contrast. There are also several chemical dye stains that are used in conjunction with cyanoacrylate and alternate light sources (see Fig. 30).

Cyanoacrylate is usually applied via evaporative fuming in a sealed or air-flow restricted chamber. A glass aquarium or similar device is usually desirable since the fuming process can be observed without interfering with the process itself.

Recently, vacuum chambers have also come into use. Since cyanoacrylate fumes are heavier than air, the fumes will tend to settle and displace air in low areas of a chamber. To prevent this uneven development, small fans are sometimes included in the fuming chambers to circulate the fumes as well as any added moisture. Moisture enhances the cyanoacrylate's chemical reaction. Utilizing a vacuum pump, most air from the chamber is removed. This vacuum environment eliminates the need for a circulation fan.

Another method of applying cyanoacrylate is with a hand-held, butane-heated, fuming wand. These portable wands allow the application of fumes to specific areas, especially useful for large items and difficult to reach places. The butane burner heats a sample of cyanoacrylate that is embedded in steel wool. The resulting fumes can be controlled for application to specific areas that may contain latent fingerprint impressions.

There is a wide variety of chemicals used in the development of latent fingerprint impressions. Various chemical formulas, may over-time, fall out of favor. This usually depends on a formula's effectiveness, ease of use, cost, or destructive properties. All chemicals require proper safety precautions, these especially, since most are intended for reactions with the residue components of human skin.

List (A) is a sample of chemicals commonly utilized in the development of latent fingerprint impressions. This list is intended to allow the reader to familiarize themselves with some of the basic development chemicals. For details on the application of these chemicals reference: *Fingerprint Development Techniques* by the Scientific Research and Development Branch of the London Home Office 1998.

A. Sample List of Fingerprint Development Chemicals

Chemical latent print developers:

• Ninhydrin (triketohydrindene hydrate) Reacts with amino acids. (Paper, unfinished wood, cardboard)(see Fig. 29)
  –Zinc chloride enhancement of faint ninhydrin stains
• Cyanoacrylate (Ethyl-2-cyanoacrylate, also known as super glue) (Plastic, wax, metals, textured surfaces)(see Fig. 30)
  –Cyanoacrylate with accelerated fuming by sodium hydroxide or heat.

- Silver Nitrate (reacts with chlorides to produce silver chloride) (London Home Office, 1988)
- Physical Developer (silver and ferric nitrate based solution for porous surfaces)
  –Mercuric nitrate (physical developer destainer)
- Small Particle Reagent (molybdenum disulfide solution)
- Sudan Black (dye stain for fatty compounds)
- Iodine Fuming (iodine crystals)
- Vacuum Metal Deposition (industrial layering process that often develops the background of a latent print impression creating a reverse contrast.)
- Multi-metal Deposition (a combination colloidal gold and physical developer process in tetrachloroauric acid solution)
  –Colloidal Gold

Chemicals used for adhesive surfaces:

- Crystal Violet (gentian violet)
- Sticky Side Powder® (powder in solution)
- Brilliant Blue R-250 (protein stain, mainly used for blood)

Photoluminescent dyes:

(For use with specific light sources and filtration)

- Rhodamine 6G(see Appendix B)
- DFO (1,8-Diazafluoren-9-one) (amino acid stain)
- Ardrox
- Basic Red 28
- Yellow Brilliance
  –Basic yellow 40
- MRM 10 (Non-porous surfaces)
- Safranin o

Blood enhancers:

- Amido Black (naphthol blue black) (protein stain)
- Leuco-Malachite Green (enzyme reagent)
- Luminol (not recommended for fingerprint development)

While luminol's chemiluminescence is often sufficient to locate blood, it is not suitable for the development of fingerprint impressions in blood(see Appendix B)
• DAB (diaminobenzidine)
• Brilliant Blue R-250 (protein stain)
• TMB (tetramethylbenzidine)

2. LASER/ALTERNATE LIGHT SOURCE (FORENSIC LIGHT SOURCE)

The use of lasers in detection and identification of materials, including latent print impressions, came not long after the invention of the laser in 1960. The term LASER is an acronym for Light Amplification by Stimulated Emissions of Radiation. Lasers and alternate light sources are coherent lights of specific energies (color) and bandwidths (purity of color). Many alternate light sources are adjustable in energy output and band-widths.[1] White light, for example, is made of a combination of all colors.

These coherent light sources often have the ability to create contrast in a latent print simply by applying a specific energy of light. The latent fingerprint or dye-stained fingerprint absorbs specific light energy and then emits new light at a lower energy level. This lower energy fluorescence type light is called photoluminescence. The difference between the absorption and the emitted light energy is called the *Stokes-Raman shift.* By optically filtering all the light except the dye stains fluorescence, contrast is increased.(see Appendix B).

In many cases, a latent print is latent simply because its fluorescence is too faint and is not visible within other incident light. Think of a room full of 1000 talking people; it is very difficult to hear just one. Yet, if you could filter out most of the other 999 voices, you could then hear the one person you wish to hear. This is a similar to the concept that applies to developing latent fingerprints with laser or alternate light sources in conjunction with optical filters.

The adjustable alternate light source uses a single white light source that is often of the arc type. Using different color transmit-

---

1. Most alternate light sources (forensic light sources) only have the ability to emit usable light in a single bandwidth. Thus, not all colors are reproducible, as some colors are the combination of more than one distinct bandwidth.

Sample flow-chart of dye-stain development.

Light source emits coherent or narrow bandwidth blue light.

↓

Latent fingerprint and/or dye-stain absorbs blue light.

↓

Latent fingerprint and/or dye-stain emits light
at a lower energy such as orange.

↓

Latent fingerprint is viewed through orange optical filter.
Orange filter absorbs ambient blue light allowing orange
fluorescence to pass to eye or camera.

Figure 31.

tance and bandwidth filters outputs can vary from long wave ultra violet (UV) 300nm to near infrared (IR - heat) at 750nm.[2]

Electromagnetic Spectrum (Not to scale)

Gamma–X rays–Ultra violet–(visible)–Infrared–Microwave–TV
–Radio
Visible = (Violet, Blue, Green, Yellow, Orange, Red)
Visible colors combined = White light

The human eye is only sensitive to the visible part of the electro-magnetic spectrum which is about 380nm to 770nm (Strobel, Compton, Current, Zakia, 1986, p. 424). This relatively narrow bandwidth is, incidentally, similar to the peak output of our local star, the Sun. Photographic film and electronic sensors, such as charged coupled devices (CCD's), can be made to record or sense emissions from other parts of the electromagnetic spectrum as well. It only goes to reason that higher energy light, such as x-ray and gamma rays, passes through our retinas, failing to behave in the expected nondestructive manner that triggers the light sensitive receptors.[3] Lower energy light also fails to interact with the receptors

---

2. One nanometer (nm) = one millionth of a millimeter (mm) or 10^{-7} cms.
3. These light sensitive receptors are called the cones and rods. Cones specialize in color, while rods sense density.

in our retinas. The same is true for the development processes as well. We need light to interact with the development process to achieve the desired results. This is why most forensic applications concentrate on ultraviolet through infrared, and latent print development techniques utilize ultraviolet through the color red.

When a dye stain is applied to a latent print residue or a cyanoacrylate developed fingerprint, the stain chemically reacts with the print. Each dye stain has its own light absorption and emitting characteristics. A specific laser is selected, or the alternate light source is set to emit the specific light the dye stain will absorb (see Fig. 31). Since the dye stain is selected to react with the latent print, these areas will generally retain more of the stain. A rinse solution is often used to prevent the background from retaining too much stain. The use of colored optical filters allows only fluorescence to be transmitted to the eye and the camera film. This process creates the needed contrast between the developed fingerprint impression and its background. This dye stain enhancement with fluorescence is called *dye-stain development* (see also Appendix B).

In the terminology of physics blue light (photons) from the light source is partially absorbed by electrons in the dye stain. The dye-stain electrons then emit photons in a new lower energy version such as orange.[4] Some of the orange light from the dye-stain and much of the blue incident light travel to our orange viewing filter. The orange filter absorbs the blue light and allows the orange light to pass. The result is that we would see the fluorescence of the stained latent print. Contrast may now be sufficient to visualize the previously latent print.

The use of lasers and alternate light source techniques is most effective in controlled low light conditions. Any unwanted light would obscure or at least reduce the contrast of the latent print in question. In the above example, any white light that was contaminating the experiment would not be completely filtered (absorbed) by our orange viewing filter. Since the dye stain could not absorb some of the other colors that make up the white light, we would view it as extraneous light that lowers the contrast of our latent print.

There are many chemical dyes on the market today. However,

---

4. "Nature always has it worked out so we never get more light out than we put in." Feynman, Richard P. 1985 *QED The strange Theory of Light and Matter* , Princeton University Press, p108.

most have applications outside latent fingerprint development. We can expect new dyes to be introduced for latent print development on a regular basis as experimenters look for more effective and efficient ways to develop latent fingerprint impressions, (See Also Appendix B for an illustration on the use of a fluorescent dye stain.)

3. SPECIAL CONDITIONS

A. Firearms

Firearms are always a difficult item on which to locate latent fingerprint impressions of identification value. However, latent fingerprints have been developed on most all firearm surfaces including barrels, receivers, grips, triggers, magazines, and cartridges. The surface texture and material of each part of a firearm will vary widely. These surfaces range from rough plastic, clean smooth metal, to heavily oiled or rusty metal. Firearms, as with most items, should always be processed under bright light conditions. Black or blued firearms make visualization of powder developed latent prints difficult. Chromed firearms act like mirrors, reflecting the color and intensity of the ambient light sources. This can also cause difficulty when attempting to locate latent fingerprints. As with all latent print impressions, the environmental conditions that the latent prints have been exposed to affect their longevity.

Cyanoacrylate fuming is a common latent print development method for firearms. Cyanoacrylate fumes react with latent print residues to create a white plastic-like print impression. A cyanoacrylate developed print can often be subject to additional developers or dye-stains. These sequential development steps are only needed if the contrast of the fingerprints is insufficient for comparison purposes after the first development process.

Standard methods of cyanoacrylate fuming and nonmagnetic powders do not affect future ballistic tests. If possible, the barrels of firearms should be blocked with small corks or similar nonabrasive plugs to prevent a cyanoacrylate film from building up in the barrel. Also, any excess magnetic powders should be cleaned from the action and barrel area of a firearm prior to any ballistics testing. Compressed air works well in removing magnetic powder adhering to metal surfaces.

Processing firearm triggers is possible and is routinely examined as part of the overall latent print search. Most triggers, aside from being small areas, are grooved to ensure a good grip is achieved when firing the weapon. Smooth surfaced triggers do offer the possibility of quality latent print impressions, yet statistically do not often yield detailed latent prints that are usable for comparisons purposes.

Cartridges (rounds) and casings (spent or empty cartridges) have very different recovery rates when it comes to developing detailed latent prints. Spent casings undergo extreme pressure with some expansion combined with high temperatures when fired in the chamber of a firearm. The probability of crime scene latent fingerprints surviving the firing process is very low. Cyanoacrylate with dye-staining is a common, if futile, development method for spent casings.

Statistically, it is more likely to find usable latent prints on cartridges. Basic powders or cyanoacrylate fuming are effective development methods for cartridges. Cyanoacrylate fuming in a vacuum chamber can even develop latent prints on cartridges within ammunition magazines. These cyanoacrylate-developed prints become chemically fixed to a more durable state and are less likely to be seriously damaged during their extraction from the magazine. It also seems that the smaller the cartridge, the lower the chance is of developing latent prints of identification value. The logic here is that a surface's area is proportionally related to successful recovery rates of identifiable latent fingerprints.

B. Human Skin

"The probability of recovering a latent fingerprint of evidential value from the skin of a dead body is approx. 15,000,000 to one", reports an older article in the *Journal of Forensic Identification* (Sampson, 1996). While it is certainly not impossible to obtain fingerprint impressions from human skin, it has proven extremely difficult in real crime scene situations. However, research has increased in this area of study. Numerous types of powders, chemicals, dyes, and alternate light sources have been tested. Some techniques have had positive and repeatable results, especially in laboratory conditions. Also, actual latent prints have been recovered from the skin of homicide victims. These victims were thought to have been touched

Thin glove layer

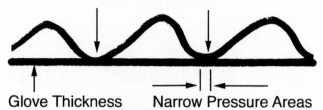

Friction Skin Pressure

Glove Thickness   Narrow Pressure Areas

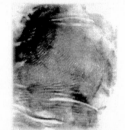

Fingerprint impression made through thin
latex glove to adhesive tape.

Figure 32.

by the perpetrator in a manner that would likely deposit fingerprint
impressions. The deciding factor in development of fingerprint
impressions from skin seems to be temperature. Current research is
studying how temperature affects latent print residues and how those
residues react with a chosen developing or transfer medium
(Sampson, 1999). It is suspected that a *readily repeatable*, crime scene
applicable, development process for human skin may never material-
ize. Yet, as techniques have improved, so have the previous fifteen
million to one odds. The odds of finding crime scene fingerprints of
identification value on a deceased victim's skin is near impossible to
calculate. Uncontrolled and undocumented variables in homicide
crime scenes prevent patterned results when analyzing detail of this
type. The point is it is very difficult to develop identifiable fingerprints on skin, even under ideal conditions. Since each case is different, a single development technique may never suffice. If such
processes were developed, the implications to homicide investiga-
tions would be significant. The problem is that the latent print must
be separated from a like surface, although the constituents of fingerprint impression residues do vary. The skin's surface is a pliable epidermis that is generally covered with many of the same residues

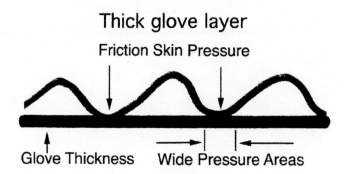

Figure 33.

found a typical the latent print, including oils, moisture, and skin cells. While it may not be as difficult as separating water from water, it is difficult due to the similar nature of the residues. Research continues.

C. Gloves

Under certain conditions, can latent print impressions be left behind while touching an item while wearing rubber gloves? Yes. Thin rubber or latex gloves may allow a transfer of pressure from the friction ridges of the fingers and palms to a surface. The glove surface may deposit its surface contamination, not necessarily latent print residues, in a reproduction of the friction skin's detail inside. Glove thickness, material construction, and surface texture will affect the transfer of a fingerprint impression(see Fig. 32).

Impressions made *through* a rubber or latex type glove may have a softly diffused appearance, as the glove will distribute the pressure of the friction ridges. Thicker gloves will yield even softer impressions. Gloves that are sufficiently thick, including leather and fabric, will absorb the slight pressure differences between the friction ridges evenly. If the pressure differences are completely absorbed, a transfer of the fingerprint impression is not possible(see Fig. 33).

Of course, the surface of the gloves themselves can be processed for latent prints. The gloves would be processed with standard contrast-enhancement development techniques. Magnetic powder is often used on rubber and latex surfaces. Other chemicals and stains may also work. Both the inside and outside of a rubber or latex glove could be processed. Most rubber gloves will turn inside out as they are removed from the hand. As found, the exterior would most likely have been the surface that was in contact with the friction skin of the hand.

While gloves of leather and fabric do not transfer friction ridge impressions, they can be considered evidence from other aspects of identification.[5] All leather and fabric surfaces are unique in themselves. Comparisons may be possible if sufficient detail is present in the developed glove impressions.

D. Extreme Weather Conditions

It is common for identification personnel to statistically recover more latent print impressions from evidence during the warm months of the year as compared to the colder months. It seems that sweat glands are more active in the warm months allowing more residues to be available to cover the surface of the friction ridges. Also, a reduction in the recovery rates of latent print residues in cold weather may be partly because cold air has less capacity to carry moisture. High humidity is a known enhancer of many latent fingerprint processing techniques and humidity levels drop in the cold months.

The freeze-thaw cycle also adversely affects latent prints, especially when associated with condensation. The residue of latent prints *may* be fragmented by the condensing moisture and expansion by ice crystals. While it may sometimes be possible to see and develop an impression after these processes have occurred, the ridge characteristics and other identifiable details are often lost.

While weather extremes can affect latent print impressions, there is no sure way to tell whether a latent impression is actually degraded to unidentifiable levels unless development attempts are made. Even short-term submersion in water does not necessarily destroy a latent print. Any oils of the latent print residue may not be immediately dispersed or dissolved by the solution. It seems there is a parallel in the science of fingerprints to the quantum physics concept of uncertainty. With latent fingerprints, you can only be sure of what you

---

5. Latent fingerprints have been developed on tight weave fabrics. Latent fingerprint impressions made in blood or other contaminants may increase the possibility of developing detailed fingerprint impressions.

have, not of that which you do not! Since we would not know the true nature and composition of any latent print impressions, we cannot predict how weather and extremes will affect the permanence of a print itself. We must actually attempt the development to see whether a detailed fingerprint impression is present.

4. FUTURE OF LATENT FINGERPRINT DEVELOPMENT

Standard contrast-enhancing development powders have been in use since the concept of latent fingerprint development was first conceived. Laser and alternate light sources (forensic light sources) have only been in use since the technology was available to make the special glass coatings used in transmission and barrier filters. However, it is slowly being realized that most current development processes rely on there being sufficient residues to interact with powders, chemicals, or light. If the residues are not sufficient to interact with these processes, it does not mean that latent prints are absent.

Spectroscopy may be the future of so-called latent print development. Remember that latent print development is simply a contrast-enhancing process. Spectroscopy methods allow one to analyze the surface contamination (residues) and plot them out on a graph. "With rare exceptions no two molecules have identical infrared and raman spectra" (Fateley & Bentley, 1991). Currently, only small areas can be analyzed at a time. Yet, with the frequent doubling of computer processing power every few years, in the near future, we can hopefully expect the capability to analyze large surface areas for latent prints with relative efficiency. The surface contamination could be mapped in two dimensions thus allowing the user to delete all compounds except that residing in the latent fingerprint residue. In this manner, artificial contrast is achieved by substance identification, rather than visual contrast enhancers. This may lead to the realization of reliably identifying latent fingerprints on the skin of homicide victims.

Chapter 7

LATENT FINGERPRINT
QUALITY VARIATIONS

1. LIFE EXPECTANCY OF LATENT FINGERPRINT
IMPRESSIONS

Determining the age of a crime scene fingerprint could often eliminate doubt about whether the print is relevant to the specific crime. It is common knowledge in the field of identification that there is no reliable way to determine the age of a latent fingerprint *outside* of standard physical means. These standards include, but may not be limited to, these following standards:

Known Time Standards for the Deposition of Fingerprint Impressions

- Date of an item's creation or manufacture. Fingerprints cannot be deposited on something that does not exist.
- An item's acquisition or transfer date. A previously inaccessible item may have been relocated or generally made available to fin gerprint access. This may include newly purchased items or goods brought in from other areas.
- Known or limited access times to an item or surface. Some items or places may only be accessible at certain times or in certain condi tions. This could include timed safe locks or even extreme weath er conditions that prevent or disclose access. Lack of shoe prints in the snow may limit access to area prior to snow's fall.
- Witness and/or surveillance evidence. Eyewitnesses may provide information as to when access was made or was available.

• Last thorough cleaning of item or surface. Thorough cleaning will eliminate oil and moisture based latent fingerprint impressions.

Beyond these standards, the science of placing specific time lines on latent fingerprints breaks down due to the many uncertainties regarding the conditions of deposition. Just one uncertainty can be sufficient to undermine any known time being placed on a latent fingerprint application. However, an experienced fingerprint specialist may be aware of many time-related factors in developing latent impressions. Many processes are chosen based not only on surface texture and conditions, but on time as well. For instance, if the latent prints that are in question are from a burglary that has happened within a few days, then one may choose powder development processes that are affected by moistures and oils in latent print residue. If the crime in question is considerably older, then other processes such as chemicals may also be considered.

On cases that are weeks to months old, etched prints would also be documented. With etched prints, the oils and other chemical compounds in the latent print residue have chemically reacted with the surface of an item to form a semipermanent and often visible impression. Placing a time on when a fingerprint impression was made is not an exact science as many variables can affect the process. Yet, sometimes etching can be used as a time guide. If a robbery had just occurred, it would be highly improbable that any etched prints found on a cash drawer would be relevant to the case.

Some latent print impressions can last for decades or longer. Fairly recently, war criminals have been identified from original WWII documents.[1] Forensic lighting techniques and various chemicals have enabled fingerprint examiners to examine evidence that might have previously been considered of no value. The latent print residues may have specific absorption and reflectance characteristics that allow contrast enhancement of the historical latent fingerprints (see also Chapter 6, section 2).

The scientific study on latent print durability has proven to be very difficult. This is because controlled experiments are hard to compare to the real world's unknown conditions. Thus, time is seldom a concept that latent print examiners can testify to. The fact that a latent print impression was found and that a fingerprint identification was,

---

1. Essentially, some latent prints could be termed as permanent as they may be as durable as the surface on which they reside.

or was not, affected is usually the extent of latent print testimony. Any known time standards will vary by case, and these standards are generally outside the testimony of the fingerprint expert.

It should also be noted that there is no proven way to tell gender or race with latent or inked fingerprint impressions. Statistically, one race or group of people may have a higher percentage of certain pattern types as compared to another group, yet this cannot be used as an identification tool since the same patterns would also be found in another population, just at a different statistical average. The actual identifying characteristics such as the spatial relationships of ending ridges and dividing ridges of friction skin is not at all distinguishing among various populations. To the fingerprint expert, all people are created equal, yet are unique in their details.

The age of a person is another factor that cannot be accurately deciphered from latent fingerprints. Due to the size variability of people, small fingerprints do not always belong only to young people. It is impossible to tell the age of a person by their fingerprints, except possibly in the cases of very young children and infants. From about six to nine years of age, the size of the human hand is not much different from that of a small adult.

2. NO LATENT FINGERPRINTS IMPRESSIONS FOUND

The concept of making an identification from latent print impressions requires that certain requirements be met. These requirements are a specific chain of related events and conditions that are applicable to the latent fingerprints themselves. Without these related events, it may not be possible to develop fingerprint impressions to use in comparisons.

Conditional Requirements for the Possibility of Latent Fingerprint Comparisons and Identifications

1. A latent print impression of sufficient detail must be present on the surface of the item in question.
2. The sufficiently detailed latent print impressions must be attainable by current development technologies. Also, the chosen development method must be compatible with the surface type

and texture on which a latent print may reside.
3. Print developing processes must sufficiently develop the latent prints.
4. Exemplar fingerprints must be available for comparison.
5. A qualified latent print examiner must be available to make a comparison with the exemplar prints and subsequently offer his/her opinion.

If any of these conditions are not present, a fingerprint identification cannot be made. Statistically speaking, identifications made from crime scene latent prints are uncommon. Of the millions of thefts and burglaries that occur every year, only a small fraction meets the above requirements. It is very common to find and/or develop latent prints that lack sufficient detail that prevents an identification from being made. It is also common to have quality latent fingerprints but to never identify their source. Also, a fingerprint specialist may be of the opinion to say that an item or surface might have been touched in some manner, but it is unknown as by whom, and that it was during an undetermined time frame. The fragmented and unidentifiable friction ridges that are developed on a surface may make this determination. Although the developed prints may be of no identification value, it may sometimes be said that evidence does exist that shows the items were indeed handled.

Was an item touched or handled? Items touched by friction skin do not necessarily receive detailed latent fingerprint impressions. Conditions for deposition of detailed latent fingerprints are not always available. These conditions may include the items in the following list.

No Fingerprint Impressions of Value Were Found on the Surface in Question

- The item or surface was not touched in a manner sufficient to deposit or remove residues creating a latent fingerprint impression.
- No latent fingerprint or surface residues were available for transfer or interaction.
- The item was not touched or handled.
- The chosen development processes could not develop the latent print impression. Also considered here is the fact that development

processes are constantly being improved.
- The surface texture and or porosity does not allow the application of a detailed latent print impression.
- The fingerprint specialist failed to develop or discover existing latent fingerprints.
- The item, surface, and/or fingerprint residue has undergone a destructive man made or environmental change since latent print impressions were deposited.

In most cases, the reason why a latent print impression was not developed is simply a matter of speculation. Since the latent print cannot be viewed if it does not exist, experience is often the only reliable source to understand *possible* reasons why a latent print was not found.

3. FINGERPRINTS WITH INSUFFICIENT DETAIL FOR IDENTIFICATION

Both developed latent fingerprints and inked fingerprints have a quality threshold beyond which confident identifications can no longer be effected. Each fingerprint specialist evaluates a fingerprint for detail, clarity, and degree of distortion. Also considered is the psychological aspect of vision, such as the brain filling in details which may not exist. This is commonly called closure in Gestalt psychology[3] (Stroebel, Compton, Current, Zakia, 1986, p. 430). With fingerprint identification it would seem prudent to have at least a basic understanding of Gestalt psychology as it relates to vision. An example would be a fragmented friction ridge that is smoothed out or filled in by normal the eyebrain interaction. It is our brain that organizes the information gathered by our eye, thus forming an understandable mental image. These images do not always accurately reproduce reality.[4]

Fingerprint impressions that do not rise above a relative quality threshold are appropriately labeled; insufficient detail for identifica-

---

3. Gestalt psychology describes many vision perceptions, and includes the principles of grouping. These include similarity, proximity, closure, and continuity.
4. Color blindness is also of concern with regards to fingerprint identification. Pseudoisochromatic color vision testing is available to detect some forms of this vision impairment. Latent print impressions can come in a variety of colors, or developed with a color of visual light ranging from violet to red.

tion. Although a pattern type may be recognizable, it may lack sufficient information to be used in comparisons for identification. Each fingerprint specialist will evaluate fingerprint impressions as they prepare to make a comparison. Once a fingerprint has been labeled insufficient detail for identification, there is little chance of resurrecting the fingerprint for future comparison. This is part of the verification by peers' process that is so vital to accuracy in the identification field. This fingerprint quality threshold is not a fixed equation. Each fingerprint must be evaluated individually, while keeping in mind that accuracy is the goal of every fingerprint identification. Accurate fingerprint identification information allows the criminal investigation to progress. If a fingerprint identification cannot be confidently made then none should be attempted. Statistically speaking, the fewer characteristics present or confidently visible, more likely a false identification could be made. Fingerprint specialists are well aware of this indefinable boundary between identifiable and nonidentifiable fingerprints.

In summary, an evaluated fingerprint impression can be one of three quality levels. These quality levels determine the comparative value of a fingerprint impression.

Three Quality Levels for Fingerprint Impressions

1. The fingerprint is of good quality and detail. A fingerprint identification may be possible.
2. The fingerprint is not of identification quality, yet certain features, such as shape or pattern type, may be visible. This may possibly allow for an elimination comparison. This type of quality level may be labeledas insufficient detail for *identification.*
3. The fingerprint is of no value. No reliable or unique information is available for evaluation. This may be labeled; insufficient detail for *comparison.*

Elimination comparisons are comparisons that seek to exclude specific fingerprint impressions as having not been made by a particular source. However, elimination type comparisons are often of little relevance to a crime scene. This is due to the fact that, in most cases, little is known about an item or a surface's history. Also, the fact that a person's fingerprints are not developed on a particular surface does not necessarily mean that the surface was not touched by that person.

It should be noted that even if a latent or inked fingerprint impression was originally indicated to be of identification value, this does not mean a fingerprint identification can or must always take place. In fact, it is not uncommon for a fingerprint specialist to decide that no identification can be made after having compared the fingerprints in question. Once a comparison is attempted, it may be decided the latent print or the inked exemplar prints lack sufficient detail and/or clarity.

Chapter 8

FINGERPRINT IDENTIFICATION

1. CONCEPTS OF FINGERPRINT IDENTIFICATION

For thousands of years, the identification of individual persons has relied on facial recognition. This system works well for family and friends, yet it is insufficient for most other applications. Even photographic portraits are of little use in our world of 6 billion people.

A wide variety of identification schemes have been invented, with an ultimate goal to individualize the human individual. Fingerprints have proven to be one solution. Fingerprinting as a popular means of identification has been in use since the 1900s. It was quickly realized that a simple, inexpensive, and reliable means of identification had been found. A century later, there seems to be no need to replace fingerprint identification with DNA or eye retinal scans as a *simple* means of identification.

The spatial relationships of the fingerprint's characteristics, also termed points, or minutia, do not change from embryonic development until death's decomposition. While injury and disease can amputate or obliterate localized areas of friction skin, any remaining area can still be used for identification. While most people think of an individual as having ten fingerprints, actually, most persons have only four friction skin sources. These include the two palmar surfaces with fingers, plus two planter surfaces. The friction skin on the palms and feet is essentially continuous from the tips of the fingers or toes to the wrist or heel of the foot. Normally, the friction skin is interrupted only by tension creases and flexion creases. Frequently, the friction skin on the sides of the finger and palm continues uninterrupted around these various creases (see Fig. 49). The main reason we think of ourselves as having ten identifiable fingerprints is that most inked exemplar fingerprint impressions filed in databases only record impressions of the last joint on the 10 fingers.

The basis for fingerprint Identification is summed up with this excerpt from an *FBI Law Enforcement Bulletin*: "The positive nature of fingerprint identification is based on the following two facts which have been established through observation for many, many years: 1. Every finger of every person bears a ridge arrangement which is unique. 2. Barring cases of accidental or surgical removal, this pattern is permanent for life of the individual and endures until decomposition of the skin after death. These statements are also true of the ridges on palms of the hands and on the toes and soles of the feet" (FBI, 1978).

This is the general foundation for identification from fingerprints, yet more specifically, we should note that not all the human population has fingerprints as we have described them earlier in this book. Since fingerprints are a genetic trait, some persons do lack normal friction skin. It seems, however, that this genetic condition is *extremely* rare. The author has only seen one case of this genetic deficiency. In place of the normal friction skin was a soft padded skin lacking any recognizable friction skin, yet containing several times the normal amount of creases. The soles of the feet were said to be of the same type of skin. Any identification of this type of skin would have to follow rules of comparison identification that apply to tool marks, tire, and shoe impressions. With this special skin condition, it is unknown how the pores in the palmar surface have been altered due to the lack of friction ridges. The sweat pores are normally found on the ridges themselves.

For normal friction skin identification, the spatial relationships of the ridge characteristics are compared to a known print such as a 10-print fingerprint card. The characteristics include ending ridges and

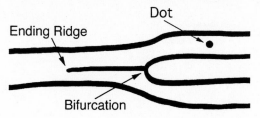

bifurcations that are also called dividing ridges.

   Combinations of these two types of characteristics create grouped characteristics. These grouped characteristics are useful when comparing large quantities of similar type patterns. The spatial relationship rules of fingerprint identification still apply when comparing grouped characteristics.

A. Common Friction Skin Characteristics

(Characteristics are also known as points of identification or minutia. Repeated from Chapter 2 for convenience.)

A. *Ending ridge.*

B. *Bifurcation* (Dividing ridge).

C. *Dot* (Extremely short ridge being as long as it is wide).

D. *Enclosure* or Lake (Two close and connected bifurcations).

E. *Trifurcation* (A true trifurcation would be one ridge dividing into three, yet most all examples are actually two very close and connected bifurcations that share on ridge).

F. *Short ridge* or island (Two ending ridges connected by a very short ridge).

G. *Right angle intersection* (Separate ridge intersection common in cores of loops, tented arches, and palmar thenar areas.) Some Right Angle Intersections are called ridge connections or crossings. Also, some types of crossings may actually be forms of bifurcations.

H. *Bridge* (Connected bifurcations sharing one ridge).

I. *Spur* (Combination of short ridge and bifurcation).

J. *Triradius* (An intersection of separate ridges often found in the delta areas. A triradius is similar in appearance to a bifurcation yet, with a greater angle between the separate ridge intersections).

These are some of the most common types of characteristics and characteristic groups that a fingerprint specialist encounters during routine fingerprint comparisons.[1] Some of the characteristic names are used interchangeably, such as island, enclosure, eye, and even short ridge. This is understandable since some features are their negative image in reversal type impressions. Fingerprint identification does not require two positive images for comparison. A negative image is often the result of the background being developed rather

1. There is no maximum number of individual characteristic types. As noted in the list, many of the characteristics are variations and groups of simpler characteristics.

than the latent fingerprint ridges(see Reversals, later in this chapter). Most identification terminology attempts to utilize layman's terms for simplicity. Since the intended audience is not expected to be familiar with anatomical terminology, investigators and jurors should encounter minimal fingerprint jargon.

For the comparison of characteristics and their spatial relationships, a fingerprint specialist will attempt to find an unusual group or set of characteristics in the unknown print. The known print is oriented in a normal viewing position if possible. This normal position is the usual way a fingerprint specialist views fingerprint impressions. Even palms have major features in their shape and details that allow, in most cases, a fingerprint specialist to locate which area of a palm the impression originated from. Using these shapes and characteristic groups, a comparison with known fingerprints can take place. If a particular area of the known prints is similar in appearance, then a more detailed comparison of the individual characteristics and their spatial relationships will take place. Keep in mind that the detailed comparison of fingerprint impressions is often made with the aid of a small, specially-designed, magnifying glass. Sharp metal pointers are often used to mark characteristics as a fingerprint comparison progresses. These pointers help the fingerprint examiner compare specific characteristics without loosing their place among many other characteristics. These pointers and characteristics are viewed through the magnifying glass.

Some elements of the fingerprint impression are evaluated before comparisons are even attempted. To make an identification, a developed latent print or an ink print must be sufficiently clear and detailed, and characteristics must be present. Once this is established, the examiner will evaluate the shape of the fingerprint impression which includes ridge orientation and ridge flow or direction.

The Basic Steps for Fingerprint Comparsions

1. Evaluation of friction ridge flow or direction.
2. Orientation of print is possible. Most print impressions are viewed with the tips of the fingers up and the wrist of the palm being down.
3. Identify pattern type if applicable. When working with prints made from the last joint of the fingers, pattern types are often identifiable.

A specific pattern type only needs to be compared to like pattern types with similar shapes.
4. Evaluation and comparison of the spatial relationships of available characteristics.
5. Evaluation and comparison of ridge structure, creases, and pores if available and necessary. Large representative areas of friction skin impressions will undoubtedly contain sufficient ridge characteristics that further detailed evaluation would be unnecessary.[2]

If comparisons of the prints cannot be easily accomplished due to poor quality exemplar prints, then those identifications should be postponed. Once clear and detailed exemplar prints are made available, comparisons can then be made. Usually, it would not be logical to attempt unnecessary comparisons with substandard grade exemplar prints. The risk is not so much an increased likelihood of making a misidentification, but rather that actual identifications may be overlooked.

Fingerprint comparisons are made, and identifications are effected, by comparing the spatial relationships of characteristics in two separate impressions. Statistically, a single or even several ridge characteristics are an insufficient foundation to effect a fingerprint identification. The reason is that it is too probable that these small samples could be reproduced with the same relationships. However, as more characteristics are added to the comparison, the odds of finding a matching, nonidentical sourced, friction skin impression decreases. This decrease is practically, but not quite logarithmic. In addition, the fingerprint specialist can also consider edgeology and poroscopy in their low characteristic count comparisons.

Thus, there is no foundation for a minimum number of individual characteristics when effecting a fingerprint identification. A minimum number such as 12 or 14 is not a foundation for accuracy. Verification of fingerprint identifications by experienced peers is the only means to effectively minimize errors. "The adoption of a low minimum standard would tend to give people of limited training in the field confidence in establishing identification on small numbers of characteristics which they would not otherwise have attempted" (FBI,

---

2. Ridge structure evaluations may also include distortions, and the overall reproduction quality of the latent print. The reproduction quality of a fingerprint may limit some of the ridge structure's identification value.

1972). The advent of computer-made, human-less identifications, may be the turning point with non-contested fingerprint identifications. Currently, most fingerprint identifications are not contested in court. Nonverified computer matches will likely have a higher error rate. Would human-less computer identification systems need to use a minimum number of characteristics to ensure a reasonable degree of accuracy? It is doubtful that computerized systems will ever match the accuracy of an experienced and verified fingerprint specialist.

While many countries do not have minimum requirements for the quantity of identifying characteristics, the lower the number of characteristics, the less likely an identification can or will be effected. Also, the lower the overall quality of a print impression, the more likely it will be classified by a fingerprint specialist as unidentifiable. However, once a print is labeled unidentifiable with insufficient detail, it does not always mean that it will retain that label. It is also not unheard-of to change the status of a print impression after reexamining its attributes. It is also possible that electronic or digital photography enhancement technology may clarify a previously unidentifiable print.

There is a threshold beyond which fingerprint identification can no longer be made. This threshold is always on the mind of the fingerprint specialist while fingerprint identifications are being effected. However rare, a fingerprint identification can be changed from positive match to a negative match after verification by peers. This could be the result of several factors, including a paperwork error or a misidentification. Yet, another possibility is that an evaluation by a more experienced examiner determines that one of the prints used in the comparison lacks sufficient detail for any confident identification to be made. It is important that the fingerprint specialists have sufficient experience when comparing low characteristic count impressions. Due to variabilities in any two identical sourced latent prints, the specialist must make sure that they are not explaining away legitimate discrepancies. For this reason, it is important that latent print comparisons are made from the latent print to the exemplar print. This ensures that only the clearly-defined characteristics are used in a comparison.

The friction ridge characteristic's degree of distortion and clarity will be considered by the fingerprint specialist to determine whether the two impressions are from an identical source. If the spatial relationships of the comparison prints do not match, then no identification can be made. Remember that the palmar friction skin is continuous from the tips of the fingers all the way to the wrist. This may require the fingerprint specialist to compare more than just the last joint on each finger. After comparing all possible locations between the unknown and the known prints, a determination will be made of either match or no match found. This determination will be the opinion of the fingerprint specialist. The next step in the fingerprint comparison process is to have the comparison fingerprints peer reviewed. Whether an identification has been made or not, comparisons are best forwarded for further review. It is not uncommon for another fingerprint specialist to find an identification that has been previously overlooked.

Possible Conclusions Resulting from a Fingerprint Comparison

• No match was found.
• Identification. (The impressions compared are from an identical source.)
• Incomplete. (Major case prints needed for further comparison.)
• Fingerprint impression is of insufficient detail for identification or comparison use (see also Chapter 7, section 3).

Major case prints are known inked print impressions of friction skin areas that are not found on a common inked fingerprint card. Areas of friction skin such as extreme sides and tips of fingers and palms may be required to complete a comparison between known and unknown fingerprints. Poor quality known inked prints may also cause missed identifications or incomplete conclusions (see Chapter 4, section 1).

A conclusion of "no match found" is sometimes changed after securing a better set of inked prints for comparisons, or in a case where a positive match was simply overlooked. When the proper orientation of a small print impression is not known, comparisons become more difficult. A reversal, or negative latent impression is also a major cause of overlooked identifications (see also "Reversals" later in this chapter). Another factor in the "no match found" scenario is the fact that while some print impressions lack sufficient detail for identification, they can sometimes be used for elimination purposes. An example would be if an item could have only recently been available for fingerprint deposition. Consider, for instance, the inside surface of a double pane glass window broken in a burglary. If a latent print with a recognizable pattern or shape that is of "elimination value only" was developed on the interior surface of the window and a suspect does not posses this pattern or shape, then arguments could possibly be made that a particular person did not make the fingerprint impression. Yet, if the item with the low quality elimination print was available for fingerprint deposition by persons other than the suspect, then this type of elimination print would probably be irrelevant as it could not be determined that the print impression was made during the commission of the crime. Generally, this type of elimination is often of no value to a case, however, under special circumstances it may be relevant(also see Chapter 7, section 3).

There are many aspects of the identification process that require an experienced fingerprint specialist.[3] Developed latent and inked prints are not necessarily of ideal quality. Also, latent and inked prints are *always* a fragment of a whole, and often a very small fragment. This, in combination with smudging, distortion, low contrast, reversals, and other variables, suggests that many comparisons can be difficult. The poorer the quality a latent print is, the less likely an identification can be made.

The explainable differences between two identified fingerprint impressions usually consist of scars, blisters, distortion, dirt contamination of impression, and skin and/or surface conditions (see Figs. 45, 46, 47, & 48). Sometimes even characteristics can appear to have variations, yet these too may be explainable. The most common characteristic anomaly is the bifurcation that sometimes appears as an ending ridge or vise versa. Differences in the impression's application pressure, ink, latent residue, rough skin, or textured surfaces are the common causes. When compared characteristics appear different and are unexplainable in the normal sense of distortions, or common variations, these characteristics are termed a *dissimilarity*. A Dissimilarity is a different characteristic(s) that originated from different nonidentical sources. While it is sometimes said that a print impression with 12 or 14 matching characteristics and one dissimilari-

---

3. Often the title of Specialist or Examiner does not correlate with experience. Many fingerprint experts consider that five years of actual fingerprint examination work are required to be considered as experienced

ty fails to constitute an identification, this is not true. Practically speaking, a fingerprint impression with 14 matching characteristic points would not contain a true dissimilarity. This concept has been stated over and over by the FBI. The odds of this scenario would indeed be astronomical and do not warrant further discussion.[4] The correct question to ask would be are the characteristics in question clearly detailed and suitable for use in identification? However, it may be possible that a compared fingerprint contains a feature that is unexplainable in the strict sense of the word. This may be because the examiner would not necessarily know all the variables that were present during the application of a fingerprint impression. Printing pressure and surface/medium inconsistencies may cause reproduction variations. A variation is not necessarily a dissimilarity.

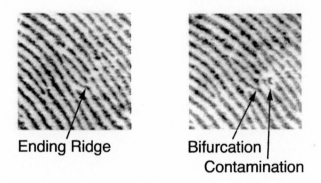

Ending Ridge   Bifurcation
                        Contamination

Figure 45. Explainable fingerprint reproduction differences due to contamination and pressure.

---

4. The point here is that properly executed fingerprint identifications are based on a foundation of solid statistics. To dwell on possibilities with highly improbable odds would be counter productive. If errors are made, they will most likely originate from improper methodology when comparing fingerprints, whether they are of good detail of lower quality, computer-generated fingerprint images. The threshold in which a fingerprint will become unidentifiable will depend on the information available in the evaluated fingerprints.

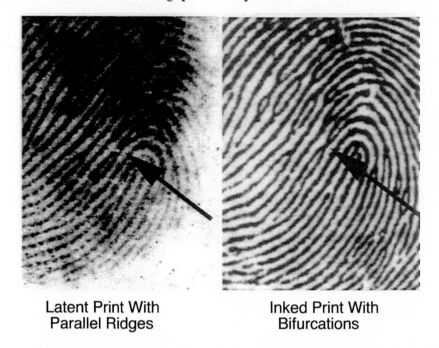

Latent Print With   Inked Print With
Parallel Ridges   Bifurcations

Figure 46. Explainable fingerprint reproduction differences due to pressure.

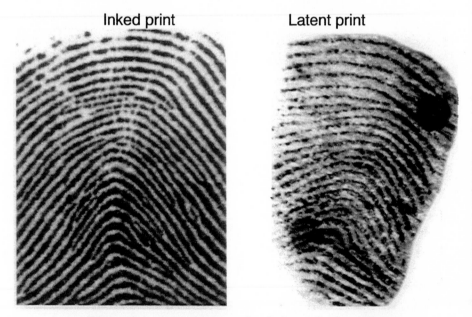

Distortion can change the "shape" of a print
Distortion can be localized or overall shape changes.

Figure 47. Explainable fingerprint reproduction differences due to distortion.

In lieu of the fact that characteristic detail can be somewhat variable in its appearance, some computer automated, fingerprint identification computer systems (AFIS) do not heavily weigh on the difference between ending ridges and bifurcations in their search calculations. In some tests on two major AFIS systems, identical candidate scores were achieved when the entire search print was searched as 100% bifurcations and again with 100% ending ridges.

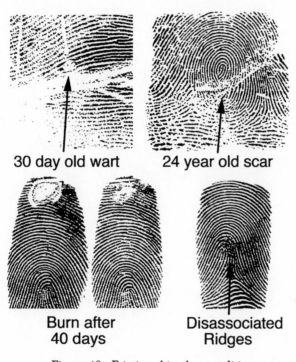

30 day old wart   24 year old scar

Burn after   Disassociated
40 days   Ridges

Figure 48. Friction skin abnormalities.

The comparison of characteristics' spatial relationships also includes the lack of characteristics in any given area. Thus, a comparison would include characteristics, characteristic groups, and lack thereof. However, the lack of characteristics is not conclusive by itself when standard characteristic based fingerprint identification methods are used. An identification from ridge impressions themselves, without using several characteristics, would require identification methods used in *poroscopy*, and *edgeology*. More information is available on these topics later in this chapter.

Palmar friction skin is continuous from the fingertips to the wrist. Creases at the joints do not always completely interrupt ridges. As shown in Figure 49, the ridges at the edge of the finger flow past the flexion joint crease.

The most commonly found areas of friction skin impressions correspond to the larger padded areas of the palmar surface (see Fig. 50). These areas also represent the areas with the largest contact areas, boldest ridges, and least amount of creases. This suggests that friction skin has some genetic adaptation relative to their form and function.[5]

Friction ridges circumnavigate the flexion crease at the finger joint.

Figure 49.

---

5. The areas of friction skin least likely to come in contact with a surface are generally found to be of fine delicate ridge detail and contain, on the average, a higher number of small tension creases.

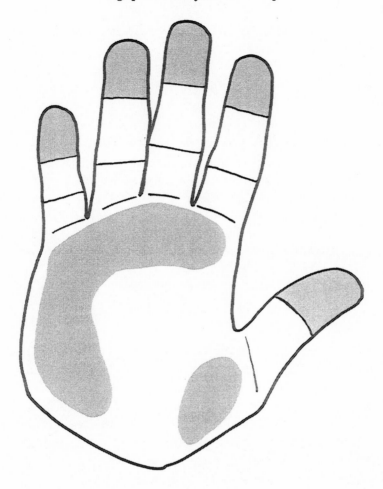

Figure 50. Common source areas for latent friction skin impressions.

The danger in latent fingerprint identification is when the specialist or examiner is willing to go beyond comparison of actual details, such as characteristics. Filling in the blanks, so to speak, is a method of making the latent fingerprint evidence match the inked exemplar fingerprint. A vivid imagination can sometimes make smears and undefined smudges and density variations into seemingly identifiable characteristics (see also Chapter 7, section 3). This lack of respect for statistical probabilities usually represents undefined identification protocols and backward comparisons. To avoid these tendencies, a fingerprint specialist will compare the developed latent print to the exemplar fingerprint. Thus, the imagination of the fingerprint specialist is constrained and Gestalt type psychology is minimized. With this correct way of identification, only the *clearly detailed* characteristics in the latent print are compared to the exemplar samples.

Most comparisons between fingerprint impressions are accomplished with inked fingerprint impressions. Usually, the inked impressions are recorded on a standard 10-print card, as illustrated in Figures 1 and 20. For the comparison of crime scene latent print impressions, the fingerprint specialist must be aware that on 10-print cards, the relative position of the left fingers is not the same as on the left hand. A 10-print card is organized for classification purposes, not for latent print comparison purposes. On a 10-print card both thumbs are placed on the left side of the card. This does cause occasional difficulties when the latent prints being compared are thought to be consecutive impressions of fingers from the left hand.

2. INCIPIENT RIDGES

Incipient ridges are another characteristic that may fall into the explainable differences category. Incipient ridges are friction ridges that are not fully formed as compared to normal ridges. These incipient ridges are often just a fraction of the height and width of a regular friction ridge. These ridges also lack the pore structure of the normal ridges. Incipient ridges have the same permanent qualities as fully developed ridges, yet they are noted for being inconsistent in their reproduction quality. For incipient ridge to be used in the identification process, they must be sufficiently reproduced in both the known and the unknown prints that are being compared.

Varying application pressures when an impression is made may prevent the incipient ridges from coming in contact with the receiving surface. The inconsistent reproduction of incipient ridges is mainly because many of these ridges are not as tall as regular ridges. The lower an incipient ridge is, compared to its surrounding fully formed ridges, the less likely it will reproduce consistently in fingerprint impressions.

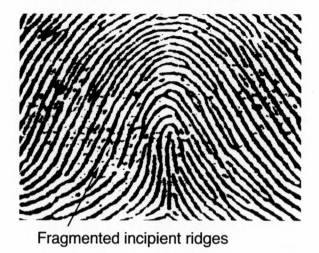

Fragmented incipient ridges

Figure 51. Incipient ridges.

3. REVERSALS (NEGATIVE FINGERPRINT IMPRESSIONS)

A reversal is a tonally reversed fingerprint impression. These reversals are also called negative impressions. Normally, the development chemicals and powders are designed to develop fingerprint residues, yet they often develop all the surface contaminations leaving underdeveloped areas in the form of a negative fingerprint image or reversal[6] (see Fig. 53).

Comparisons of fingerprint impressions can take several forms. Developed crime scene latent prints can be compared to known inked prints or other latent prints. Inked fingerprints are also compared to other inked prints. Sometimes latent fingerprints are even compared to other latent fingerprints. In our normal comprehension of comparisons with fingerprint impressions, we think that dark or colored areas represent the ridges of the fingerprint. The background of the print impression is represented as space or valleys between the darker ridges. The opposite can also be possible. With latent prints, it may be that the development powder adhered to the background rather than the print impression. Here, the background would be the dark developed area. Overall the resulting developed print looks

6. Some development techniques such as vacuum metal deposition, an industrial coating process, develops the background and does not develop fingerprints. The resulting reversal is expected.

much the same as a normal print. Yet, a reversal results from the removal of surface residues by the friction skin during contact.

A comparison with these reversal type impressions poses no problem to a fingerprint specialist as long as he or she is aware that the print is *indeed* a reversal. A reversal may not always be obvious. When comparing fingerprints, and it is found that the spatial relationships of all characteristics are off by one ridge count, and ridge endings on one print appear as bifurcations on the other print this is a clue for the examiner to consider the possibility that one of the prints in question is a reversal. Most, if not all, reversals are developed latent fingerprint impressions. Many fingerprint identifications have gone unnoticed due to the inability of the fingerprint specialist to discover that they were working with a reversal. The Rubin's figure, Figure 52, a common psychological illustration, is similar to the identification example of how the brain deals with tonally reversed images. With the Rubin's figure, one can see a candlestick as a black image or two human face profiles, nose to nose, in white with a black background. Either image is correct, as would be a negative toned impression of a fingerprint. This is termed figure-ground and is another visual concept in Gestalt psychology (Stroebel, Compton, Current, & Zakia, 1986 p. 429). Some other, possibly related, aspects of this figure-ground type dilemma are the concepts of *afterimages* and *figural aftereffects*. Afterimages can be both positive and negative toned. These negative illusionary images are attributed to the "local bleaching of the visual pigments in the retina's receptors, positive afterimages to a continuation of the firing of the visual nerve cells" after the viewers gaze has ceased. Figural aftereffects "are changes in the size, shape, or orientation of a perception as the result of a preceding visual experience" (Stroebel, Compton, Current, & Zakia, 1986, pp.418-419). While these retinal anomalies interfere very little in fingerprint identification, it would be wise to be aware that they do indeed affect vision, and possibly fingerprint comparison evaluations.

Automated Fingerprint Identification Systems are not affected by fingerprint reversals. Patterns and core placement, or center of print, do not change. Add to that, the fact that these systems do not heavily weigh characteristic types, such as ending ridges or bifurcations, a fin-

---

7. In some extreme examples the pattern may change. Since pattern classification can be determined by a single ridge count, a one count loop may be evaluated as a tented arch. However, borderline patterns are routinely referenced to other possible patterns during the print's classification. Thus, it is unlikely that this scenario would be problematic.

gerprint search would still be effective.[7] When comparing on-screen images called candidates, the fingerprint specialist would still be faced with the problem of viewing a tonally reversed image.[8] Yet, often, a high candidate score will often give a clue to the fingerprint specialist that a searched print is a reversal.

A reversal-type latent fingerprint impression is not uncommon. A partially reversed print impression is easily noticed, whereas complete reversals may be difficult to recognize. Experience does not seem to make much of a difference when it comes to recognizing reversals. Again, the ability to recognize a reversal can be likened to the black and white Rubin's figure that allows a person to mentally view a wine glass or two faces in the same image, but not necessarily both at once.

Nose to nose profiles
or vase?

Figure 52. Rubin's figure.

---

8. Most AFIS. systems allow the user to invert the displayed image to reverse image densities.

Reversals can be easy reversed to positive images with special photographic paper in the darkroom, or with digital images by a computer software function called "invert." The resulting image is in positive form, which is desirable for courtroom display.

Inked print   Latent print

Figure 53. Reversal or negative impression.

4. POROSCOPY, EDGEOLOGY, AND CREASES

Based on the concept that no two tangible objects are identical except in source, close inspection of friction ridges reveals pores and uneven ridge edges. These details are identifying features in themselves. Thus, the next step beyond ridge characteristic-based fingerprint identification is *poroscopy* and *edgeology*. Poroscopy is the study of the pore structure on the ridges of the friction skin. Edgeology is the study of the edge structure of the friction skin ridges (see Fig. 54). This concept of the closer you look, the more differences you will find, is not new. Even the art community is utilizing this concept to record the authorship of important works of art.

It is reported that friction skin contains about 2700 pores per square inch (Olsen, 1978, p. 30). Also, the edges of friction ridges themselves constantly vary in size and shape. Thus, spatial relationships of the pores and ridge edge detail can lay a foundation for identification similar to tool marks or shoe impressions (see Fig. 54). Yet, there may be little need to go to these reductionistic extremes for an exclusive means of identification. Most fingerprint specialists realize that poroscopy, edgeology, as well as ridge orientation are already incorporated into fingerprint identification. Unfortunately, the reproduction of pores and edge detail of the friction skin ridges is unreliable at best. Many modern laser jet printers used in the printing of live-scan-type fingerprint cards do not have the resolution to adequately reproduce this extreme detail (see also Chapter 4, section 2 and Appendix C).

Another identifying feature of palmar and sole friction skin is creases. Major creases called *flexion creases* allow the skin to fold on to itself to accommodate hand or foot articulation. Smaller *tension creases* are also present in various shapes and sizes (see Fig. 55). The palmar surface, excluding the fingers, generally has at least three larger flexion type creases. These creases flow away from the thumb starting in the area below the index finger. The top most crease is called the distal transverse crease and flows horizontally across the palm. In the middle is the proximal transverse crease. The third major crease is the radial longitudinal crease. This crease outlines the thenar area near the thumb (Cowger, 1983, p. 60). The joints of the fingers contain additional flexion creases, Unfortunately, creases like ridge edges, are not always unchanging over time. As the epidermis layer of the friction skin is subjected to various conditions, such as abrasion, the detail of creases and edges of the ridges may temporarily change. Some creases may also be sensitive to a person's weight variations. These inconsistencies make the use of creases as a tool of identification most difficult. However, creases do play an important part in identifying from which part of the palmar surface a developed latent print fragment might have originated. Creases from different locations of a palm often have features such as shape and relative orientations that allow a fingerprint specialist to clue in on a specific area of friction skin during a print comparison. These crease features will often allow the examiner to orientate the latent print itself so as to speed up any comparisons. The standard orientation of a viewed palm is to have the tips of the fingers as up and the direction of the wrist as down.

Creases in the skin may also be a permanent feature. Most tension creases are merely minor folds or indentations in the epidermis layer. However, in some flexion creases, the crease structure itself is dermis layer deep. This dermis foundation precludes any ridge structure. In some cases, it can be noticed that flow of the ridges is affected at the boundary of these flexion creases. In Figure 55, the flexion crease in the interdigital palm area below the little finger(middle arrow)causes a major interruption of the ridge flow. Thus, it is reasonable to assume that some of the flexion creases are indeed dermis layer genetic formulations and not exclusively products of skin folds or tension.

Generally, poroscopy, edgeology, and creases do not play a large role in fingerprint identification. However, when a fingerprint identification contains very few identifiable characteristics, the value of these secondary identification factors is proportionally increased. Essentially, a fingerprint identification of just five characteristics would (should) be substantially supported with additional characteristics with poroscopy, edgeology, and/or creases. In fact, as less ridge characteristics, such as bifurcations, are used in a fingerprint identification more poroscopy, edgeology, and/or crease detail *must* be used[9] (see also Chapter 11, section 1).

Figure 54. Pore and ridge edge structure.

9. Each fingerprint identification is an evaluation of all available fingerprint information. Thus, each fingerprint comparison will be unique in its own details.

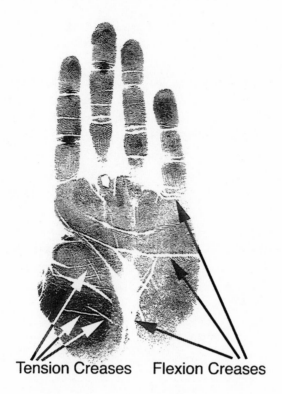

Tension Creases   Flexion Creases

Figure 55. Flexion and tension creases.

5. COURT PRESENTATIONS AND QUALIFICATIONS

The ultimate goal of any fingerprint identification is to provide information in the form of personal identification. When this identification becomes material and relevant evidence, illustrative displays are often used to covey this information to the court. A presentation of these displays provides an illustration of technique and/or findings of the fingerprint specialist. Court presentation of fingerprint evidence is usually presented in one of two types. First, there is a simple verbal description of the fingerprint identification process, fingerprint evidence, and expert opinion of the fingerprint specialist. This is often accomplished utilizing generic fingerprint illustration charts. Generic charts are sometimes used when fingerprint evidence plays a minor role in a case or when someone needs basic fingerprint information to better understand testimony. The second type of presenta-

tion utilizes enlargements of the actual fingerprints that were used in
the fingerprint comparison. These comparison charts can be photographs mounted on cardboard, or photographs projected onto a
screen (see Fig. 56). Fingerprint charts illustrate the comparative
aspects of a fingerprint identification. Photographic enlargements of
exemplar prints and the corresponding print it was compared with
are shown side by side. The second print can consist of either another inked fingerprint or a developed latent print, depending on what
types of fingerprint impressions were actually compared.

The comparison chart is generally entered as evidence, allowing it
to be viewed at later times. Yet, sometimes, the comparison chart is
not entered as evidence and is simply used as an illustration by the
fingerprint examiner. Here, the charted fingerprint evidence would
not be available for future reference by juries or investigators.

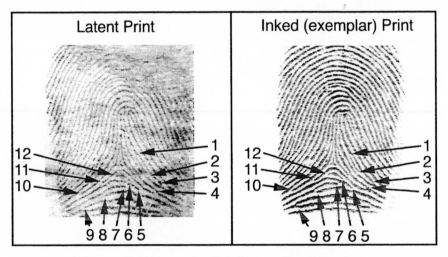

Figure 56. Fingerprint identification illustration chart.

Minimum educational and experience qualifications for the hiring
of a fingerprint specialist vary greatly between agencies. The require-
ment may simply be a high school diploma or GED, driver's license,
and 21 years of age. Other agencies may require an AA, bachelor's
degree, or a minimum amount of experience in a related field of
study. Most fingerprint training relies on state and FBI-sponsored
programs, as well as on-the-job experience. Many fingerprint specialists are also trained in criminalistics and photography, as well as fingerprint identification. Recently, several colleges and universities

have started offering study opportunities in fingerprint identification.

There is no government-regulated certification for the identification of fingerprints. The identification field has several informational-type organizations, and some have made available their own certifications.[10] Historically speaking the identification field's self regulation has proven exemplary.

Some jury polls by the FBI have revealed some interesting notions of what may be expected of a fingerprint specialist. These polled juries overwhelmingly believe:

- ". . . that fingerprint experts should belong to an association related to their field of study"
- ". . . fingerprint experts should work in a crime lab" (Illsley, table 13).
- ". . . fingerprints are the most reliable means of identifying a per son" (Illsley, table 5).
- ". . . a fingerprint expert should have another expert verify his/her work before he/she testifies in court" (Illsley, table 20).

In fact, most fingerprint specialist do work in lab environments, do belong to informational associations, and do have their work verified by their peers. Verification is the foundation of the identification process that keeps errors to an absolute minimum. Subsequently, a very low error rate with fingerprint identifications keeps the quality reputation of the fingerprint specialists intact.

---

10. Some of the identification and forensic organizations have certifications not only in fingerprint identification, but also in areas such as; crime scene processing, trace evidence analysis, photography, tool marks, shoe impressions, and tire impressions.

Chapter 9

FINGERPRINT FABRICATIONS, ERRORS, AND EVIDENCE

1. FABRICATION OF FINGERPRINTS AND IDENTIFICATION ERRORS

Ideal conditions for latent fingerprint testimony are one of accuracy and honesty. The identification field has many safeguards available to help prevent false information from entering the evidence chain. It is paramount that personnel management keeps these safeguards effective. Standardization and continuous training are the key to, and foundation of, effective crime scene fingerprint processing and the resulting fingerprint identifications. Overall accuracy of fingerprint identifications is the result of experience, in combination with, the verification process. A fingerprint identification should always be verified by a qualified fingerprint specialist.[1] A crime lab or identification bureau's reputation for quality work is largely based on the verification process. Lack of verification on any crime scene fingerprint identification should be unacceptable and should open questions as to why the verification standard was not utilized.

Latent fabrications have been documented; however, statistically, they are rare. Although a law enforcement fingerprint specialist is employed for the prosecutor, the main product of an identification bureau is information. This information is obtained from case evi-

---

1. There is a difference between ink and latent crime scene type fingerprints. The difficulty level in effecting identifications with latent fingerprints is generally much greater due to their lower average quality. Therefore, latent print identifications must always be verified.

dence, and the concept that the evidence speaks for itself is the guiding factor in all fingerprint comparisons. Speculation is not synonymous with fingerprint identification work. If a developed latent print has insufficient detail a fingerprint identification cannot be made.[2] Whether identifications resulting from fingerprint comparisons help or hinder a prosecution should be of no concern to the fingerprint specialist. When processing crime scenes and fingerprint evidence, identification personnel are usually unaware of most case details. It is common knowledge that many fingerprint identifications, generated from crime scene evidence, belong to persons unrelated to the crime itself.

Recovered fingerprint impressions are generally not compared to suspects at the scene of a crime. Controlled conditions of lighting and equipment are often needed for fingerprint comparisons. It is also common to process much of the crime scene evidence for fingerprints under these controlled conditions. Transportable items of evidence are best processed under laboratory conditions. Since latent print development is a contrast enhancing technique, proper lighting and/or chemicals may be needed.

While the vast majority of identifications are accurate, there are the rare cases of fabrication, errors, or misidentifications as they are related to the evidence. The following list outlines several types of conditions that may result in a fabrication or what seems to be a false identification[3].

Fabrication of Fingerprints and Identification Error Possibilities

- Latent fingerprint impressions of subject *intentionally planted* at a crime scene by unknown persons. This may include fingerprint bearing objects transported to scene.

---

2. New DNA techniques have brought fingerprint identification and DNA identification down to the same level, in that latent fingerprint residues may contain DNA information. However, cross contamination is more likely with DNA technology than with fingerprint identification. It is quite rare to transfer existing latent print impressions to another surface while maintaining the necessary detail to effect an identification. Also, most transfers of latent fingerprints yield mirror images of the original.

3. Seemingly false identifications are those in which accurate identifications have been effected from unintentional or irrelevant persons to a crime scene. It is not always possible to be aware of what evidence has been touched, when, and by whom. Nor, is it always possible to remember what we have touched as handling objects or touching surfaces is often a subconscious act.

- Latent fingerprint impressions of subject *unintentionally* transported on items that were left at a crime scene. Also, most crime scenes occur in areas that have had some degree of human access. These areas may contain fingerprint impressions unrelated to any crime.
- Latent or inked fingerprint impressions *created* (fabricated) from manufactured evidence, or wrongfully duplicated from existing fingerprint impressions.
- *Errors* in evidence labeling during or after evidence processing, and/or photography.
- Intentional *misrepresentation* of fingerprint evidence.
- Identification error, unintentional *misidentification* of a fingerprint.

Intentionally or unintentionally deposited fingerprints may arrive at the crime scene on portable evidence. It is important to understand the relevance of all evidence involved, as well as known time lines for that evidence. It is important to realize that identifications effected from fingerprint evidence made by an unknown suspect is not a misidentification, nor is it a crime on the part of the fingerprint specialist. The fingerprint specialist simply forwards information discovered through fingerprint identifications. The investigators and subsequently the courts decide whether fingerprint evidence is material and relevant.

Latent fingerprint *lateral transfers* are also a possibility. The primary medium of a latent fingerprint transfer is adhesive tape and plastic. The adhesive of tape may readily accept fingerprint residues. These residues can then be transferred as the tape is applied to another surface and subsequently removed. Nonporous smooth plastic and glossy paper has also been known to transfer latent fingerprint impressions. This type of transferred fingerprint will be a mirror image of a regular inked impression of the same finger. A mirror image fingerprint impression may be very difficult to recognize and may often go unidentified.

While outright fabrications of fingerprint evidence are very rare, evidence documentation errors are more common. Most common documentation errors are discovered as inconsistencies in the collected evidence, documentation of evidence, and in the evidence chain itself. These should be the first places to look for discrepancies on a suspected misidentification. Areas where errors can be introduced into the evidence may include the following

Possible Error Introductions with Latent Fingerprint Identifications

- Numerical data or other data entry errors (clerical error).
- Improperly marked or misidentified evidence. Original crime scene photography, and or videography may help clarify evidence questions.
- Misidentified photographs of latent print impressions. Photographic sequence should also include overall views of areas where latent print impressions were developed and photographed. Photographic logs correlating negative frame numbers, and/or ID tags in the photographs should be used to ensure accuracy.
- Improperly marked latent lift cards. Basic case information must be added to the cards at the time the lift was made. Basic case information for latent lifts should include:

    1. A detailed description of the latent print lift location.
    2. Date lift was made.
    3. Officer making lift.
    4. Address of incident.
    (see also Fig. 28)

- Crime scene contamination due to the unintentional introduction of irrelevant evidence. It is not always possible to discern which evidence is relevant to a crime scene.

In reference to the above item regarding latent lift cards, adding this information at time of processing can help eliminate simple documentation errors. Adding this basic information to latent lift cards, after other items have been processed, could prove difficult if not irresponsible. When multiple items or cases have been processed for fingerprints, there is the risk of mixing evidence information, not to mention individual cases. Since many crime labs have a heavy workload, the crime lab often resembles a production line of latent print processing. Because of this, it is *paramount* that basic information is added at the time the latent is preserved as a lift and/or photograph.

Frequently, the background of a latent lift or photograph provides information aside from the lift itself. It is sometimes possible to trace latent fingerprint lifts back to their original lift locations. This extra background detail may help validate a print lift's authenticity. This

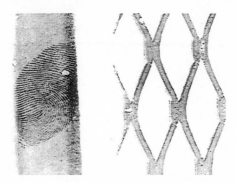

Figure 57. Sample of screen texture in a crime scene latent fingerprint lift.

extra detail is often background information as texture patterns (see Fig. 57). The texture pattern should be fairly consistent between the evidence surface and the latent lift.[4] While latent print lifting tape does not always reproduce the surface texture of an object with great detail, major features and general patterns may sometimes be recognizable.

Many fingerprint specialists will actually include as much background information as is convenient. Not only does this help authenticate their latent lifts, it may help locate exactly where the latent lift was made and possibly its orientation.

2. CHAIN OF CUSTODY

The fingerprint specialist receives crime scene evidence for latent fingerprint processing in a variety of ways. Each method should be well documented to ensure the integrity of the evidence. This evidence integrity is very important regarding trace evidence. Each time custody of the evidence is transferred to another person the time date, and names of persons involved should be documented. This information may be required in court to prove the authenticity and condition specific evidence.

The following list contains examples of how evidence is typically

---

4. Use of photographic filtration methods and specific light wavelengths (colors) can be used to filter-out some background patterns. This is intended to add contrast to the latent print itself. Some digital imaging filters are designed to minimize or eliminate background patterns. These electronic filters seek out repetitious background patterns and select them for removal. Removal of a background pattern will often allow for better visualization of the fingerprint itself.

made available for latent print processing. A chain of custody may be as simple as a photograph of a non-movable object or complicated as in multiple custody changes as evidence is routed to the crime lab.

Fingerprint Evidence Processing Locations and Transportation Options

- Evidence is processed and documented at crime scene.
- Evidence is recovered at crime scene and transported to crime lab by fingerprint specialists.
- Evidence is recovered by field patrol officer and transported to crime lab for processing. The custody of the evidence is then transferred to the crime lab.
- Evidence is recovered by field patrol officer and transported to property storage facility. Subsequently, the evidence is transported to crime lab at a later date.

It is important that the evidence that is received by the crime lab is correctly packaged and identified. This ensures against contamination, damage, and unauthorized handling. Most small portable items can be packaged in paper and sealed to prevent the unintended introduction of latent prints and other trace evidence. Paper packaging, such as paper bags, allows for the evaporation of moisture. This reduces the possible degradation of the latent fingerprints. Existing seals should be left intact if possible, and evidence should be resealed after processing.

When a latent lift of value has been developed, recovered, and documented, the processing officer should include his/her identifying mark on the evidence if possible or record its description. The identifying marks are often achieved by scribing or with indelible inks. Photographs of the evidence are also useful to investigators as they may clarify latent fingerprint lift locations and the condition of the evidence itself.

It is also important to remember that in some cases, public access to the evidence does not always end with the commission of a crime. Some evidence is not made available until well after a crime is thought to have occurred. Stolen vehicles, for instance, may not be found until months or years later. Numerous passengers and drivers, plus their belongings, might have had access to the vehicle. Again, latent fingerprints do not tell time, except in cases of maintained surfaces, or items with documented access times (see also Chapter 7, section 1).

Contamination of fingerprint evidence, with additional fingerprints, can be made in several ways. The most common is that of recovering officers, property facility personnel, or crime scene technicians handling items of evidence (see Fig. 58). Even with protective gloves, improper handling of evidence may destroy latent print impressions. Lifting or moving evidence by its handles is, of course, the last thing a fingerprint specialist would want. Commonly handled areas of an object are likely to posses latent fingerprint evidence. Each item of evidence is best packaged individually. It may be possible to package some evidence items together as a single item when they are like items from the same location. However, like items from different locations cannot be packaged together. This may reduce the informational value obtained from any subsequent fingerprint identification, as it may be impossible to decipher the original location of the crime scene evidence, thus, its relevance to the crime scene.

When drug residue tests and/or other trace evidence collection are to be performed on an item of evidence it is imperative that these tests are done prior to any fingerprint processing. Trace evidence, other than ballistics or tool marks may be destroyed, lost, added, or otherwise contaminated by the fingerprinting process. Latent print powders and their application brushes are almost always contaminated with various drug residues and foreign hairs/fibers. As drug paraphernalia and other evidence are processed, cross-contamination is expected. Thus, performing other tests prior to fingerprint processing eliminates the negative consequences of cross contamination.

Magnetic type powders are designed to be reused until the ultrafine developing particles, within the larger carrier particles, are depleted. Stray hair/fiber, drug residues, and even biological hazards will accumulate until the powder is replaced. Non-magnetic powders do not lose their effectiveness over time, and are used until the entire supply is depleted. This allows considerable time for the accumulation of various contaminants. However, it is not uncommon for a fingerprint specialist to replace the used bushes and powders after contacting a biological or chemical hazard.

Typical Crime Scene Evidence Flow Chart

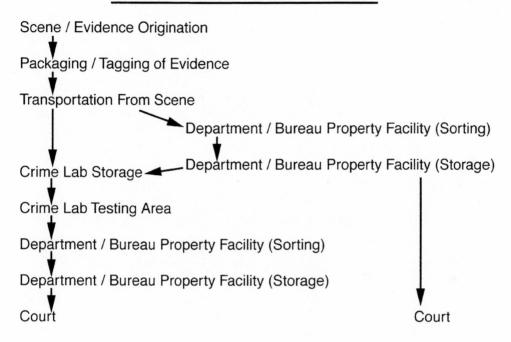

Scene / Evidence Origination

Packaging / Tagging of Evidence

Transportation From Scene

Department / Bureau Property Facility (Sorting)

Department / Bureau Property Facility (Storage)

Crime Lab Storage

Crime Lab Testing Area

Department / Bureau Property Facility (Sorting)

Department / Bureau Property Facility (Storage)

Court

Court

Typical Latent Fingerprint Evidence Flow Chart

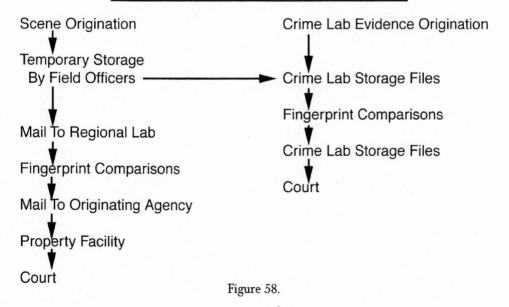

Scene Origination

Crime Lab Evidence Origination

Temporary Storage By Field Officers

Crime Lab Storage Files

Fingerprint Comparisons

Mail To Regional Lab

Crime Lab Storage Files

Fingerprint Comparisons

Court

Mail To Originating Agency

Property Facility

Court

Figure 58.

3. VERIFICATION BY OUTSIDE EXPERT

While hiring an outside expert to verify crime scene or other inked fingerprints is somewhat rare, some cases or conditions may warrant this step. The key is to ensure that each fingerprint identification made with latent fingerprints has been verified.[5] This is a protocol standard and *should* be a mandatory practice in the Identification field. Unverified latent fingerprint identifications should be suspect. Both the prosecutor and the defense can make requests for fingerprint verification by peers or by and outside expert.

Inked fingerprints are sometimes treated with slightly less suspicion. This is due to the fact that the comparison of inked fingerprints is generally accomplished with highly detailed fingerprints of good overall quality. Fingerprint specialists are often called to court to offer their opinion on inked fingerprint comparisons without the need for verification. Of course, this testimony is based on their expert opinion that is founded on experience and a history of accurate fingerprint identifications.

In a world full of "experts," it seems easier to claim expert knowledge than to provide expert testimony. This common notion is exaggerated in the fingerprint identification field. Only persons who have years of real-world experience as a fingerprint identification expert should be considered to for the verify fingerprint identifications. Experience and proper training are necessary to be an effective and accurate fingerprint expert.

---

5. Verifications should be made from the original fingerprint impressions if possible. However, good quality notarized copies of inked fingerprint 10-print cards may suffice. For latent prints the originals, as well as, any photographic enhancements should always be evaluated. Some friction skin detail is often easier to evaluate in enhanced photographic form.

Chapter 10

PHOTOGRAPHY, IMAGE ENHANCEMENT, AND COLOR

1. PHOTOGRAPHY (TRADITIONAL AND DIGITAL)

Photography, as it relates to dactylography, is a permanent means of documentation for crime scene locations, evidence, and evidence relationships. With fingerprints, the evidence would be their development and preservation, as well as documentation of the surface from which they were obtained.

Today, photographic science bridges two technological areas. First, is the light sensitive emulsion of traditional photography. While the concept of projecting images has been around for centuries, the first photograph was not taken until the year 1826.[1]

With standard photography light sensitive particles in the film's emulsion undergo a chemical change once exposed to light. This change in the film is the recorded latent image. This latent image can be preserved with special development and fixing chemicals. These chemicals allow the film's latent image to become visible and permanent.

Secondly, the computer revolution has allowed the invention of the charge-coupled device (CCD). A CCD array converts focused light into electrical signals, and subsequently computer data. In both traditional and electronic photography, images are generated from images of focused light. Essentially a CCD replaces film. A CCD also elimi-

---

1. Pinholes and camera obscuras do not utilize any type of film. These devices projected images for viewing only.

nates the need for chemicals. Electronics are used to organized the data and make it visible to the eye. A latent electronic image is essentially, a set of organized electronic data. The data is not visualized until the data is displayed on a computer screen or output to a printing device. The other basic camera functions remain similar to that of a traditional camera.

The modern digital darkroom allows a faster turnaround time from the moment the photograph is acquired to the final print visualized on a monitor or from a high resolution printer.[2] An electronic image of a fingerprint can be transmitted via modem to an identification bureau halfway around the Earth if necessary for a database check or comparison. Digital images are very similar to emulsion images in that a digital image pixel (picture element) is equivalent to emulsion-based, light sensitive, film grain.[3] The major difference is that each pixel is separately adjustable from a mode of off, or one of hundreds, thousands, or million of different colors. Conventional film is seriously limited in comparison. High-resolution digital cameras and storage devices are available as an alternative to traditional photographic methods of documenting fingerprint evidence. Digital imaging's ease of use and speed makes computer-based imaging desirable in the law enforcement field. Digital imaging also allows faster image access and distribution. The main holdback in converting to all digital imaging has been the expense of high-resolution cameras and high-capacity storage devices. Now agencies can show that traditional processes involving emulsion based-film, processing chemistry, printing paper, and darkroom machinery is increasingly more expensive. Converting to a digital system may actually save money.

With digital imaging, a person may immediately think of image *manipulation,* yet the real benefit is for image enhancement. Image manipulation is counterproductive with fingerprint identification. The goal is to identify persons from their fingerprints. Bad data such as image manipulation do nothing to further this goal. Image enhancement and manipulation have been around since the invention of photography.

---

2. The term "darkroom" is no longer applicable when referencing digital photography. Yet, analogies are made with the traditional darkroom were images are produced. In comparison, the term "filter" still has applications with both absorption and transmittance of light as well as the organization of computer data.
3. Our eye's equivalent to electronic pixels are the 20+ million rods and cones that convert light energy to usable signals from our brain.

Digital images can be adjusted or enhanced from data information that might have been obtained from outside our vision's spectral limits. Also, photographic film is available in a wide range of spectral sensitivities. For fingerprint and evidence work, three film sensitivity ranges are available. These sensitivities includ ultraviolet (UV), panchromatic (visible colors), and infrared (heat). In forensics, infrared film is mainly used in gunshot pattern residue photography. Some development dye stains do fluoresce in the infrared, yet it is difficult to work with infrared film and so; infrared applications are generally avoided. Pan-chromatic films are available to reproduce images in color or black and white. Black and white film responds to the various colors by representing them as densities of gray as the silver halide emulsion grains are exposed.[4] Color film uses multiple dye layers to form a color image. The image is formed as colors are absorbed or transmitted by each successive dye layer.

The difference between photographic enhancement and manipulation is that enhancement *does not* add new information to the existing image. With enhancements, the specific emulsion or pixel densities are adjusted darker or lighter, and patterns are minimized or removed to enhance the contrast between a latent fingerprint and its background. Manipulated images do add new information to the fingerprint image and these manipulated images have no value for identification purposes. Inaccurate information will not assist in fingerprint identifications. It is imperative that the enhanced fingerprint impression remains representative of the original crime scene fingerprint. This representation is in reference to the actual fingerprint itself. The background of the fingerprint is, of course, often adjusted to allow maximum contrast for the print.

All image enhancement should be done to a copy of the original and not to the original itself. For court purposes, it is still the responsibility of the photographer to qualify an image as being an enhancement or a true and accurate representation of the original scene. Manipulated images would not qualify.

Some law enforcement agencies have special software that can authenticate original digital fingerprint images via encryption codes. The enhanced image of a fingerprint can be compared to the original at any time. Once saved with encryption codes, the original cannot

---

4. Black and white (dye)-based film is also available. These special films allow the user to process the black and white film with standard C-41 color negative developing chemistry.

be modified, only deleted. This allows for a proper chain of custody if the original image is only available in a digital format.

Filters used in electronic image enhancements are simply software programs that mimic regular photographic filters. They also have additional features used to control image data, or minimize background patterns. These filters can be used in combination with one another to make a fingerprint image usable in a comparison or display. An enhancement of latent prints is not to make the fingerprint look more pleasing to the eye; it is to make the identifiable characteristics sufficiently clear so fingerprint comparisons can be made.

Certain film types used in combination with different colored filters can often enhance the contrast of a latent fingerprint relative to its background. Photographic filters allow their own color to be transmitted to the film, while absorbing other colors to various degrees. Depending on the reflection, transmission, and absorption characteristics of the developed latent fingerprint impression and its background, colored filters may be used. This is especially true with black and white film. Drastic contrast adjustments can sometime be made with the combination of black and white film and certain photographic filters (see Fig. 59). Colored filters used with color film are for color balance correction, as well as, contrast enhancement. Color photographic film is color balanced to reproduce colors under specific light sources. As light sources vary, color correction filters can be used to compensate for these color shifts. Most amateur color film is balanced for daylight conditions.

Black fingerprint on
orange background.
- Red filter -

White fingerprint on
orange background.
- Blue filter -

Figure 59. Contrast control with color filters and black and white film.

Lighting is also a factor to latent fingerprint enhancement. Different lighting techniques will yield different clarity or degrees of definition in a latent fingerprint. Some lighting techniques can even change the tonal values of a latent fingerprint's ridge detail so that the fingerprint becomes a reversal or negative image. This is due to the surface and the latent print's light reflection and absorption variability at different angles of light incidence. The reversal of a fingerprint's density tones is also prevalent when photographing latent print impressions with fluorescing chemical dye stains that are illuminated with lasers or alternate light sources (see also Chapter 6, section 20).

A. Common Photographic Optical Filters

1. Ultraviolet absorbing filter. Absorbs unwanted stray UV light.
2. Ultraviolet transmitting filter. This is often used in conjunction with UV light sources, and quartz optic lenses for injury or medical photography.
3. Blue filter
4. Green filter
5. Yellow filter
6. Orange filter
7. Red filter
8. Infrared filter.[5]

Generally, these colored filters transmit their own color while absorbing their complementary color. The exception is the ultra violet absorbing filter, which actually absorbs only specific ultra violet wavelengths.

2. VIDEOGRAPHY

Videography's main application in the documentation of fingerprint evidence is not in the fingerprints themselves but rather in the evidence on which the fingerprints may reside. Most Modern video cameras are based on the same technology that generates digital

---

5. Ultraviolet and infrared photography require minor focus adjustments on a lens. Light of different wavelengths will come into focus at different areas relative the film plane. With the exception of quartz ultraviolet optics, most photographic lenses are designed to focus the colors violet through red. Reference your lens instruction manual for ultraviolet and infrared photography.

images in digital cameras. A charged coupled device (CCD) converts light to specific electrical signals that are then stored on a magnetic medium. Most digital imaging computer software can acquire and enhance video images along with digital photographic formats.

Video footage is essentially a group of related clips that form some logical sequence that documents a scene and its elements.[6] Editing of video footage allows the elimination or arrangement of the individual clips. Editing can also rearrange the chronological order of individual clips. Editing can be done in two different ways.

Videography Editing

1. *In-camera Editing.* Scene footage is acquired in a manner that captures clips in a logical and proper chronological sequence that is easy for the viewer to follow. Most crime scene videos are of this type. This type of in-camera editing often requires no additionalediting to prepare the clips for public viewing.

2. *Studio Editing.* Acquired videotape clips are shot in a manner or sequence that does not allow the viewer to logically follow or understand the scenes. Also, some video clips may not be suitable for certain audiences or may not qualify for courtroom display. An edited tape is prepared from the original footage that allows the viewer to logically follow the recorded events in chronological order. This studio edited video tape is in *addition* to the uncut original. Any studio edited taped must be marked as such. Studio editing is accomplished with either video editing equipment or a suitable computer with video editing software. The original video must be preserved as evidence and should remain available for viewing.

3. COLOR

The topic of color as it relates to latent fingerprints is best thought of as a contrast adjuster. The color itself is not important, but rather its contrast ratio in relation to a fingerprint's background. The higher the contrast ratio of a fingerprint, the easier it is to see and compare

---

6. The term "footage" is derived from the historical measurement of movie film in increments of feet. Today, video lengths are measure in time.

with other fingerprints. A latent fingerprint's contrast might be increased or decreased depending on the following factors:

Contrast Variability Factors

• The ambient light sources's color and band-width (wavelengths/range of colors).
• The light absorption characteristics of the latent fingerprint and its background.
• Camera filter and camera lens absorption and transmission characteristics.[7]
• Spectral sensitivity and contrast characteristics of the photographic film emulsion or CCD.

A latent print's true color is relative to its light characteristics and the light source's color. Objects do not have color unless they are illuminated by electromagnetic radiation. In other words, the lack of color is black. In the case of light itself, its color is derived by its wavelength or combination of several wavelengths. Green light plus red light will make yellow. In the case of the reflected color yellow, such as a banana, it is understood that the banana reflects green and red while absorbing other the other colors of white light.

In the real world, we can see this effect when viewing scenes under certain colors of light. For instance, under a sodium vapor street light a dark blue car will appear, and actually is, black. Most objects are assigned their color, i.e., a blue car, when viewed under white light. In the 1660s, Isaac Newton of Cambridge University discovered that white light is a combination of all individual colors.[8] A surface's color is a product of its absorption, transmission, and reflection characteristics when viewed under a specific light source(s). A mirror or chrome surface is a surface that reflects almost 100% of the visible light that radiates onto its surface. This reflected light is in a nondiffused form. These mirror and chrome surfaces do not have a color in

7. Photographic camera lenses are generally coated with special materials to minimize UV light and unwanted reflections generated from the lens surface itself. Specialized quartz lenses are available for special application of UV light photography, as quartz optic readily transmit ultra violet light.

8. The term "white light" is only in reference to a combination, or additive mixture, of visible colors such as blue, green, and red, to make white. However, a light source may contain other wavelengths of the electromagnetic spectrum in addition to the visible white light.

themselves but can reflect the light source's color.   The poet Elliott Allen Baade takes a physics/pseudo-philosophy approach with; "A white horse has faith that he can reflect all colors" (Baade, 1998, p. 42) (see also Chapter 5, section 3).

Most light sources do not emit light only in the visible part of the electromagnetic spectrum. The sun itself has a very wide spectrum. Fortunately, most of the harmful short ultra violet wavelengths are absorbed by the ozone layer of our atmosphere. The sun's longer, lower energy infrared wavelengths, keeps us warm.

Normal incandescent light sources, such as a 75-watt tungsten filament bulb, emit the majority of their energy as heat. We see some of this bias as an orange-red cast in amateur photographs illuminated by incandescent lights. Daylight, as filtered by the sky, is generally blue-green biased, yet it varies greatly with atmospheric conditions and time of day.

Chapter 11

COMPUTERIZED FINGERPRINT DATABASES

1. AFIS (AUTOMATED FINGERPRINT IDENTIFICATION SYSTEMS)

The computer age has allowed the storage, management, and retrieval of large amounts of data that was previously not possible. Fingerprint data, such as inked prints, have been accumulating for about 100 years. The popular Henry system of hand filing fingerprint cards was being stretched beyond its efficiency limits. Automated Fingerprint Identification Systems (AFIS) computers were first introduced in the mid to late 1970s. AFIS computer databases allow the computer to do all the file searching, and it does so with an incredible time savings. Computerized files also allows for adjustable search parameters. Date of birth is one of these parameters. These parameters could also be used to electronically purge very old records in order to keep the database efficient. The Henry filing system does not allow for easy file maintenance. These manual systems needed human intervention to remove out-of-date-records. Another advantage of an AFIS database is its ability to search single fingerprints against millions of similar pattern types. The Henry fingerprint filing system was designed to search 10–print cards to other 10-print cards, not individual fingerprints. In the past, suspects were often needed before any comparisons could be made. While it is possible to hand search Henry fingerprint files for an individual fingerprint, it is extremely impractical. A hand search could consist of thousands or millions of fingerprint cards with each card bearing ten finger-prints. While in special cases, hand searches for individual finger-prints were done, the modern computer is magnitudes more efficient.

Considering that each person has ten fingers, an AFIS computer requires that each finger is assigned a pattern type.[1] Each of the ten fingerprints, with its pattern designation, is filed under one identifica-tion number. Thus, each 10-print card contains ten individual files with the same identification number. Any match to one of the finger-print files reveals the unique identification number. This identifica-tion number is cross-referenced with a person's name and other relat-ed personal information.

Fingerprint pattern types that are used as database search parame-ters can vary among the different manufacturers of AFIS computers. Typically, a condensed form of the Henry system is used. If the pat-tern type is known, then only that pattern type needs to be searched. If the pattern could possibly be interpreted as another pattern type, then the fingerprint would be searched against more than one pattern type. A scar or unknown pattern type is searched against all pattern types. Some systems can even assign pattern types automatically. The idea is to speed up the data entry process. If the computer has chosen all pattern types correctly, then the user simply accepts the input and launches the fingerprint database search. The IAFIS, or integrated automated fingerprint identification system, also uses a standardized classification system that is also founded on the tradi-tional Henry pattern classification rules. The IAFIS is a new AFIS network that will standardize the exchange of fingerprint database information (see Fig. 60).

A. AFIS and IAFIS Classification Patterns

AFIS Classification Patterns

1. Arches (plain arch and tented arch) = A or T
2. Left slope (slant) loop = L
3. Right slope (slant) loop = R

---

1. When a pattern cannot be determined, a default pattern is assigned. In the case of AFIS classifications, the "scar" pattern is designated. The scar pattern type is generally used for obliterated, unrecognizable, or unknown fingerprint patterns.

4. Whorls (plain, central pocket loop, double loop, accidental) = W
5. Scar (unknown or obliterated pattern) = S
6. Amputation = X
(See also Chapter 2 for more information on pattern types.)

IAFIS Classification Patterns

1. Arches (plain arch and tented arch) = AU
2. Left slant loop = LS
3. Right slant loop = RS
4. Whorls (plain, central pocket loop, double loop, accidental) = WU
5. Scar (unknown or obliterated pattern) = SR
6. Unable to classify = UC
7. Amputation = XX

AFIS computers are simply computers that specialize in sorting files. An AFIS computer will generate a *candidate list* of possible matches. This candidate list is based on the computers mathematical models with the 1 candidate being the most probable match found in reference to the unknown search print.[2] Subsequent candidates on the list are less likely to match according to the information processed by the computer during the search. A fingerprint match or hit does not always reside in the first position on the candidate list. Due to many variables, such as quality of the impressions in the fingerprint database and the variables in a fingerprint that is to be searched, it is possible that no match will be found. Essentially, a quality database is needed to ensure effectiveness of a computerized fingerprint search.

AFIS databases serve two main purposes. One is for inked exemplar fingerprint searches, and the second is for crime scene latent fingerprint searches. For inked print searches, inked 10-print cards are searched against the database(s) to determine if an existing record is already on file. This is called a 10-print to 10-print search. Hits against an existing fingerprint file help ensure that duplicate subject records are not created. A person's name has no value during a search of an AFIS database. No name information is needed for a searched. All that is needed is one or more fingerprint impressions.

---

2. The most probable match is in reference to the computers ability to calculate probabilities based only on the information that was available.

If the pattern type of the search fingerprint is known, then the computer need search only like pattern types. If all ten finger pattern types are known as with a 10-print card, then only like files need to be search by the computer. By narrowing down the search parameters in this way, considerable time is saved and accuracy is improved.

A computer search of the fingerprint database with a developed latent print impression obtained from crime scene evidence is called a latent to 10-print search. The searched latent print impression may only represent a very small section of a finger's ridge detail. Any hit or match would determine a matching file, thus, the identity of the individual. The absence of a hit could be due to several possibilities. Essentially, it cannot always be determined why a search of a fingerprint did not hit, only the fact that it did not.

Possibilities for No Fingerprint Match Being Found in a Database

- No matching database file exists. Most databases only represent a small segment of the population.
- No match was found due to a poor quality database or search file. This could include a latent fingerprint tracing with an incorrect interpretation of the latent print. Some systems require that latent fingerprints be traced in some manner in order for the computer to easily recognize the ridges and characteristics. Tracing of fingerprints prior to scanning (input) is an art that requires practice and precision.
- Database fingerprint file or search file contains informational errors.
- Actual match was overlooked or not recognized. Although a set of fingerprint impressions may be identical in source and in their characteristic's spatial relationships, each impression will appear somewhat different due to reproduction variabilities.
- Computer malfunction. Some malfunctions that affect search accuracy may not be immediately apparent.
- Searched fingerprint may contain search parameter errors that prevent the information from being matched. Parameter errors may include: age range, sex, fingerprint pattern type, or even an incorrect size of scanned fingerprint. If the computer system requires a 5 times enlargement of a latent print for input scanning, and a 7 times enlargement was scanned, the maximum tolerance may be

exceeded.
• Computer error during automatic fingerprint pattern classification. Some systems will automatically assign the search print a pattern type. It is possible that the computer assigned pattern type and the actual database pattern type may differ.

AFIS computer systems are manufactured by several companies. Now, almost all major government agencies utilize computerized fingerprint search technology. Of the major companies manufacturing AFIS hardware and software, each of the systems works on similar principles. Electronically-scanned fingerprints, and palmprints on some models, are run though a software program that uses mathematical computations, such as algorithms, to quantize the fingerprint information. Candidate lists are arranged in order of probability that is based on the quality of detail in the searched fingerprint. Of course, this similarity or probability is derived from the mathematical computations executed by the software. The software itself is designed to compare the spatial relationships of fingerprint characteristics. This, of course, is similar to the way a fingerprint specialist would attempt a fingerprint comparison. However, AFIS computers do not make identifications. Technically speaking, computer software cannot consistently list a search candidate match as number one on a candidate list. So essentially, a true fingerprint identification cannot yet be made by computers. Acceptable probability of a fingerprint match would take on a new meaning if computers were allowed to make routine fingerprint matches. The reason is that computers would generate a much higher misidentification rate, thus, seriously skewing statistics.

Normally, a computer's candidate list is manually compared by fingerprint specialists. If a listed fingerprint candidate warrants closer inspection for possible match verification, then copies of original documents (fingerprint cards) can be requested from the agency in question by using the identification number listed by the AFIS computer. Most all individual countries, providences and states, have their own independent fingerprint databases. Many of these independent databases are now linked to form networks. This networking concept is the future of the AFIS database and subsequently, fingerprint identification(see Figure 60).

These two main functions of an AFIS computer, the 10-print to 10-

print, and latent fingerprints to 10-print searches, form the bulk of all AFIS fingerprint searches. However, most AFIS computers allow other functions as well, such as searching 10-print cards against an unsolved latent database, the unsolved latent database consists of those latent fingerprints that were previously searched against the fingerprint database with negative results. Latent fingerprints that fail to match a database file may be registered in the unsolved latent database. A registered latent print is then available for future searches. Incoming 10-print cards that are found not to be in the database are considered to be new to the system. These new cards can then be searched against the unsolved latent database. The concept being, that a matching 10-print file might not have been in the AFIS database at the time of the original latent fingerprint search. Thus, a 10-print card search against the unsolved latent database could be found to match a crime scene latent fingerprint that was entered years before.

Modern AFIS technology is moving away from the *human* verified candidate list and toward a concept of acceptable probability automated identification. For instance, a patrol car or security system with a fingerprint-scanning device scans a person's fingerprint; this print is then digitized and sent to an AFIS computer or other software. The search results are then made available by the computer. These results can be presented in a probability list. In the case of a security access type application, a low probability on the first candidate would likely be insufficient for access. The results may or might not have been, verified by a trained and experienced fingerprint specialist. Generally, it seems that new technology is usually acceptable until proven otherwise. The field officer relies on search results to be accurate, and the information will determine the officer's course of action. It would be very unfortunate if over time, the highly accurate system of human verification is replaced with the acceptable probability of computer-generated fingerprint identification. Errors would simply be blamed on computer difficulties. Whereas, with human verified identifications, fingerprint specialists stake their entire careers on accuracy, that is 100% accuracy in fingerprint identification. Currently, the fingerprint verification process is made by experienced fingerprint specialists. This is the accuracy in the identification system.

Most fingerprint specialists are keenly aware of an AFIS comput-

er's shortfalls. It is doubtful that a reliable, humanless, AFIS computer system will replace the experienced fingerprint specialist any time
soon. While these humanless (nonverified) systems have already
been designed, the stumbling block will most likely be the fact that
while a fingerprint may be identical in origin, no two individual fingerprint impressions are alike. Yes, this is true. Each time a separate
impression is made, there will be differences in clarity, distortion,
contrast, quantity and quality of reproduced characteristics.
Different pressures may also cause previously unrecorded incipient
ridges to appear (see also Chapter 8, section 2). As discussed previously, an identification is based on the spatial relationships of the fingerprint characteristics. The reproduction quality of these characteristics can vary greatly from impression to impression.[3] These first
humanless AFIS systems are most likely to attempt nonverified identifications with inked fingerprints only. Latent fingerprint identifications are another story altogether. Even the most experienced latent
fingerprint specialists are frequently challenged with difficult poor
quality latent fingerprint impressions. Also, the advent of a paperless system may hinder a fingerprint specialist's capacity to correct
any problems that are discovered. Uncorrected problems may subsequently compound errors, thus, lowering the effectiveness of automated fingerprint identification systems.

Since the fingerprint identifications are based on statistical probabilities that no two different prints are identical, it stands to reason
that the more fingerprints that are in a database the higher the odds
of finding *similar* fingerprints. These similar fingerprints will lower
that difference in a computer's search candidate's score. This intern
may lower those odds that a computer-generated fingerprint identification is located in the number one candidate position. Again, theo-
retically for a computer to make an identification, the candidate must
reside in the number one position on a candidate list. However, with
human verified identifications, this candidate position problem is
irrelevant. A database with 210 million 10-print cards would contain
2100 million or two billion one hundred million fingerprint files. The
Federal Bureau of Investigation's Identification Unit has about 210
million fingerprint cards on file.

---

3. The skin's surface condition such as dry or calloused, will also effect the reproduction
quality of a fingerprint's characteristics.

Worldwide, there are about 6 billion people that is an amazing 60 billion fingerprints.[4] Of course, no two tangible objects in the universe are identical, except in source. Yet, sufficiently similar fingerprints may cause some identification difficulties as fingerprint databases grow ever larger. This concern is primarily meant for low quality ink and latent fingerprint impressions. This quality-related problem may be even more applicable regarding the new automated identifications made by new systems now being marketed.[5] Low quality fingerprints are more difficult to compare. A difficult fingerprint comparison is in reference to impressions with a low characteristic count or unclear features. The smaller and less detailed a fragment of latent impressions is, the less information it will generally contain.

Most statistical odds based on no two different fingerprints matching spatial relationships of the characteristics are based on normal inked fingerprints, not small low quality latent fragments. Yet, even with a fictional database of 60 billion fingerprints, it is doubtful that the integrity of 10-print to 10-print *ink* type identifications would be seriously challenged. It simply behooves us to be aware of a system's limitations as well as its strengths.

If any challenge is ever made to the concept of further AFIS expansion, it would most likely be because computerized fingerprint databases have ramifications on simple fingerprint statistics. No longer are suspects always generated from local populations (Aitken, 1995). Billions to one odds are irrevocably convincing when based on a small census group. Now that suspects will be generated via nationwide computer databases, the new odds will modify the foundation statistics of fingerprint identification. Again, this is mostly relevant for identifications based on marginally detailed fingerprints with a low characteristic count. The average inked fingerprint has a very large quantity of identifying characteristics, and a palmprint has about 45 times more.

It is important to understand that there are many variables in fingerprint statistics. For instance, if one is comparing a standard fingerprint and the fingerprint's pattern type is known, the odds would

4. This 60 billion number only includes friction skin on the last joint of each finger. Not considered here is the rest of the palmar surface or the plantar surface with its ten toes.

5. Digitally-reproduced fingerprints lack much of the fine details, or nuances, that fingerprint specialist often rely on to effect an identification on low quality impressions. It is thought that one major drawback to these types of automated systems is the increased possibly that some identifications will actually go unnoticed.

change relative to the 60 billion prints as not all 60 billion would be the same pattern type. However, if the print fragment in question is very small and no pattern type can be determined, then all fingers, palms, and plantar friction skin, including toes, may have to be considered as well. Thus, as the available comparison details diminish, the size of the potential comparison references increases. The less information that is available for a fingerprint comparison, the larger the potential areas to compare with will become. This is why verification of latent fingerprint identifications is so crucial. Last is the fact that statistics cannot factor in the very fine details of fingerprint identifications. A fingerprint's ridge shape, and ridge structure, including pores, are extremely variable and delicate in their reproduction. While computer-generated live-scan and other digitized fingerprint images fail to reproduce many of these detailed nuances, properly rolled traditional inked fingerprints can still reproduce much of this detail. With the elimination of ink fingerprint impressions in new computerized fingerprint systems, many fingerprint comparisons made from low quality digital images may prove increasingly difficult (Chapter 4, see section 2).

AFIS systems are facing another challenge as well. Compatibility has always been a factor in limiting the search capabilities of AFIS users. While regional networks have been a reality for many years, large gaps between individual databases still exist. Not every AFIS computer can access all others (see Fig. 60). A new standard for compatibility has been created. Electronic Fingerprint Transmission Specification (EFTS) should, in theory, enable all future and current systems to access each other, as well as allow access to a national system. This common EFTS specification will also allow faster search times for inked fingerprints and access to the previously isolated fingerprint databases. This newest fingerprint computer search engine is known as IAFIS or Integrated Automated Fingerprint Identification System.

A.

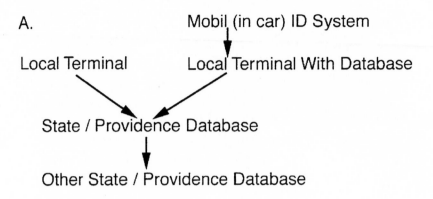

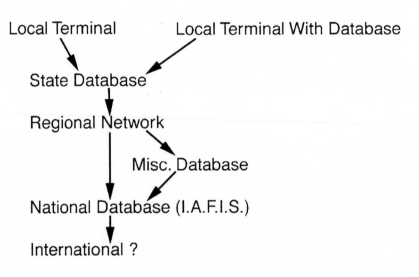

Figure 60. AFIS Networks (typical or proposed).

Each new step in computer technology has been applied to the task of matching fingerprints via electronic fingerprint databases. The systems started as localized city and state databases that helped identify repeat criminals. Now the systems have reached the national level. With national fingerprint search capabilities, state lines will loose their appeal for the criminal trying to escape detection. However, the actual value of these national systems, in terms of public safety, will be determined on how efficiently they are operated and under what or whose discretion.

Appendix A

ATTENUATION OF FINGERPRINT PATTERN TYPES

In some cases, the categorization of fingerprint patterns have been condensed and simplified from highly specific examples to a more generalized types. This is due to the standardization of manual filing classification methods, as well as computer database management of fingerprint files. Also, it should be noted that while the Henry classification system has become dominant for manual systems, most of this simplification applies to specific computer database applications. The traditional Henry classification system is a very detailed process that allows the specific grouping of like fingerprint patterns. While much of the filing aspects of the Henry system is waning, the basic pattern classification ideas are still applicable to most all fingerprint management systems including computerized systems. While the detailed Henry pattern classification system is utilized to determine if a pattern type is a whorl, for instance, a computer system generally does not require the information of what kind of whorl the pattern may be. A computer's mathematical search engine easily recognizes basic pattern shapes. Thus, over the last few decades, it seems that many pattern types have been condensed to only three or four that are utilized in computerized databases.[1] (see Fig. 61). In reality, the detailed Henry system of pattern classification is the very foundation of most pattern classification schemes whether they are condensed or not.

The NCIC (National Crime Information Center) fingerprint classification system still uses the more detailed descriptors of the Henry pattern classification system. The NCIC classification system, in essence, is a format that specifically describes what the patterns look like. For some whorl and loop patterns, this includes some aspect of pattern shape. For loops, the ridge counts between the delta and core are revealed and with whorls, the tracing between left and right delta is known. This type of system is needed when images of fingerprints are not available for comparison. A detailed description of the fingerprints will let the investigator know if further inquiries are warranted.

---

1. The total number of pattern types depends on which classification system or version is being used.

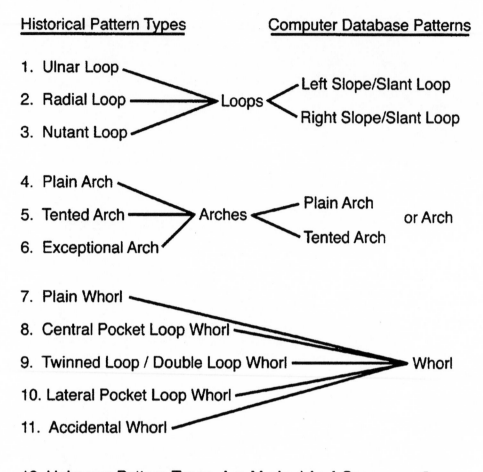

Figure 61. Pattern types (example of historical and computerized database versions).

Appendix B

PHOTOLUMINESCENCE AND CHEMILUMINESCENCE

A firearm was fumed with cyanoacrylate vapors. Here, Rhodamine 6G dye stain is used in an attempt to increase fingerprint detail faintly developed by the cyanoacrylate. The dye stain fluoresces under specific illumination and optical filtration conditions. This type of luminescence is called photoluminescence(see Chapter 6).

Figure 62. Semi-automatic pistol stained with Rhodamine 6G and viewed in normal room light.

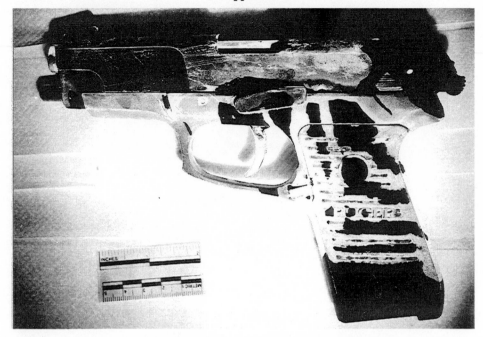

Figure 63. Same Rhodamine 6G dye-stain pistol as figure 62, now view with an alternate light source and color filter combination that are selected to maximize contrast with the dye-stain.

"Chemiluminescence is produced as a result of a chemical reaction usually involving an oxidation-reduction process. . ." (Lerner, Trigg, 1991). Chemiluminescence is different from the dye stain processes. With chemiluminescence, the chemical reaction produces the light. Luminol is the forensic scientist's main chemiluminescent agent. Luminol has applications as a blood enhancer. While luminol is not used to develop latent fingerprints in blood, it is often used to locate blood stained areas. Once located, these other chemical agents may be applied to possibly enhance any fingerprint impressions present.

Appendix C

COMPARISON OF INK AND COMPUTER GENERATED FINGERPRINTS

For the past century, printer's type ink has been the standard reproduction medium for exemplar fingerprints. Ink offers highly detailed reproductions. The limitations of ink are not in its quality, but rather in its slow and often messy application. While ink is still the reproduction medium of choice, many agencies are switching to computer-generated, live-scan-type fingerprint systems simply for its speed advantage (see Fig. 64). While lacking in finely reproduced detail, these systems do allow relatively unskilled operators to generate acceptable fingerprint images for subsequent computer database searches. With live-scan-type fingerprint imaging, each finger can be rerolled until a satisfactory image can be saved. The saved images can be printed onto standard format 10-print fingerprint cards using black and white laser printers.

Computer generated artifacts.

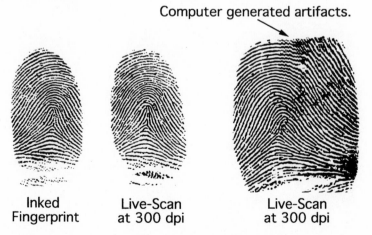

Inked
Fingerprint

Live-Scan
at 300 dpi

Live-Scan
at 300 dpi

Figure 64. Comparison of inked and live-scan fingerprint impressions.

BIBLIOGRAPHY

Aitken, C.G.G. (1995). *Statistics and evaluation of evidence for forensic scientists.* New York: Wiley, p. 132.

Baade, E. A. (1998). *Poetic theory ov justifiable ignorance.* Spokane, WA: Speculor, p. 78.

Baade, E. A. (1998). *Poetic theory ov justifiable ignorance.* Spokane,WA: Speculor, p. 42.

Berry, J. (1991). *Advances in fingerprint technology.* Henry C. Leeand & R. E. Gaensslen (eds). New York: Elsevier, page 5.

Cowger, J. F. (1983). *Friction ridge skin.* New York: Elsevier, p. 145.

Cowger, J. F. (1983). *Friction ridge skin.* New York: Elsevier, p. 60.

Fateley, W. G., & Bentley, F. F. (1991). Lerner, R. and Trigg, G., (Eds). *Raman Spectroscopy. Encyclopedia of physics* (2nd Ed.). New York: VCH Publishers, p. 1035.

Federal Bureau of Investigation. (1972). *An analysis of standards in fingerprint identi fication.* Washington, DC, p. 6

Federal Bureau of Investigation. (1978). *Identification. Law Enforcement Bulletin,* rev. 1978. Reprinted in *FBI advanced latent fingerprint school manual,* p.114.

Federal Bureau of Investigation. *Advance latent fingerprint school manual.* Department of Justice, p. 6

Federal Bureau of Investigation. *Advance latent fingerprint school manual.* Department of Justice, p. 11

Federal Bureau of Investigation. (1984). *The science of fingerprints.* Department of Justice, Rev. 12-84, p. 18

Federal Bureau of Investigation. (1984). *The science of fingerprints.* Dept. of Justice, Rev. 12-84, p. 45.

Home Office. (1988). *Fingerprint development techniques.* Scientific Research and Development Branch of London Home Office. London, p. 73.

Illsley, C. *Juries, fingerprints and the expert fingerprint witness.* Federal Bureau of Investigation Publication, Table #19.

Illsley, C. *Juries, Fingerprints and the expert fingerprint witness.* Federal Bureau of Investigation Publication, Table #13.

Illsley, C. *Juries, Fingerprints and the expert fingerprint witness.* Federal Bureau of Investigation Publication, Table #5.

Illsley, C. *Juries, fingerprints and the expert fingerprint witness.* Federal Bureau of Investigation Publication, Table #20.

Lerner, R., & Trigg, G. (1991). Luminescence. *Encyclopedia of physics* (2nd ed.). New York: VCH Publishers, p. 653.

McCarthy, D. C. (1999). Photonics gets personal. *Photonics Spectra,* Dec., p. 110-111

Olsen, R. D. Sr. (1978). *Scott's fingerprint mechanics.* Springfield, IL: Charles C Thomas, p. 30.

Saferstein, R. (1990). *Criminalistics* (4th ed.). New York: Prentice-Hall, p. 364

Sampson, W. C., Sampson, K. L., & Shonberger, M. F. (1997). *Recovery of latent fingerprint evidence from human skin: Causation, isolation, and processing techniques.* KLS Forensics, Inc. p. 39.

Sampson, W.C. (1996). Latent fingerprint evidence from human skin (part 1). *Journal of Forensic Identification,* 46 (2):188.

Sampson, W.C. (1999). *"New techniques for printing the deceased" & "Recovery of latent fingerprints from human skin."* seminars.

Stroebel, L., Compton, J.; Current, I., & Zakia, R. (1986). *Photographic materials and processes.* Boston: Focal Press, pp. 418–419, 424, 429, 430.

INDEX

A

AFIS (General), 27–28, 81, 87, 111–113, 115-119

AFIS Candidate List, 8–9, 34, 35, 113, 115–117

AFIS Network, 120

AFIS Search, 9, 14, 20, 27, 81, 87, 111–117, 119–120

Arch (general) 15-16, 17
    plain arch   15, 16, 26, 112–113
    tented arch   15, 16, 26, 87, 112,–113

B

Bifurcation (See Characteristics, characteristic types
Burns to friction skin, 14, 81

C

Certification, 93

Contrast enhancement (See latent fingerprint development and photography)

Characteristics
    characteristic types, 18–20, 70–73, 78 (excluding Edgeology, Poroscopy)
    Edgeology, 33, 75, 81, 88–90, 95
    minimum requirements, 78–79
    poroscopy, 75, 81, 88–90
    reproduction variability, 79–81
    spatial relationships, 14, 20–21, 65, 70–72, 74–76, 81, 86, 88, 114–118
    structure, 13, 28, 37

(See also Flexion creases; Tension creases)

Classification of fingerprints (general), 8, 18, 24, 27, 29, 84, 87, 114
    Henry classification system, 8, 16, 25–27
    historical classification system, Appendix A
    NCIC Classification System, 25–27
    numerical classification system, 27–28, 112

Cloning, 21–22

Contamination, 21, 46, 59, 61–62, 79, 85, 97, 95, 99–100

Crime scene search (for fingerprints), 47–48

Cyanoacrylate (See Latent fingerprint devel opment, chemical development)

D

Digital imaging (See Photography)

Disassociated fingerprint ridges, 81

Dissimilarity, 78

DNA, 3–4, 29, 70, 95

Dot (See characteristic, characteristic types)

Dye stains, 47, 51, 52–58, 105, 107, Appendix B

E

Edgeology, (See Characteristics, Edgeology)

Electromagnetic radiation, 37, 54, 109, 110

Elimination fingerprints, 31, 68, 77–78

Ending ridge (See Characteristics, Characteristics types)